A Gift

from Vis and Sally Upatisringa

in memory of his father

Hun Kwan Goh

Humboldt Library Foundation

THE RISE OF CHINA

EDITED BY Gary J. Schmitt

Encounter Books
New York   London

THE
RISE OF
CHINA

Essays on the

First American edition published in 2009 by Encounter Books,
an activity of Encounter for Culture and Education, Inc.,
a nonprofit, tax exempt corporation.
Encounter Books website address: www.encounterbooks.com

Manufactured in the United States and printed on
acid-free paper. The paper used in this publication meets
the minimum requirements of ANSI/NISO Z39.48–1992
(R 1997) (*Permanence of Paper*).

FIRST AMERICAN EDITION

LIBRARY OF CONGRESS CATALOGING-IN-PUBLICATION DATA

The rise of China : essays on the future competition /
Gary J. Schmitt, editor.
    p. cm.
Includes bibliographical references and index.
ISBN-13: 978-1-59403-231-8 (hardcover : alk. paper)
ISBN-10: 1-59403-231-9 (hardcover : alk. paper)
1. United States—Relations—China.
2. China—Relations—United States.
I. Schmitt, Gary James, 1952–
JZ1480.A57C6 2009
303.48'251—dc22   2009004138

CONTENTS

INTRODUCTION

Gary J. Schmitt

Although the United States is rightly preoccupied with the threat of Islamist terrorism and the conflicts in Iraq and Afghanistan, there is a wide consensus among American strategic thinkers that America's greatest challenge over the next decades will be the rise of China. The following collection of essays is about the nature of that challenge and what the U.S. and its allies might do in the areas of foreign and defense affairs to meet it. It is not a book that tries to cover the whole waterfront when it comes to U.S.-China relations. Nor is it a book that challenges the dominant view that U.S. policy toward China in the years ahead will continue to be a mix of engagement and hedging. However, it *is* a volume that, on the whole, points toward the need to bolster the latter half of that policy equation.

China of course is rising—even in the face of current global economic problems. Everyone is aware of the fantastic change in the country's economic situation. Hundreds of millions of Chinese have been pulled out of poverty as China's economy rockets forward, growing at a rate of more than nine percent annually now for more than two decades. Once mired in the craziness of Mao and destructive Communist attempts at "great leaps forward," the size of China's GDP is closing in on that of all the great powers of the world with the exception of the United States. Concurrent with that growth—indeed, in recent years outpacing it—has been China's investment in military modernization. The result has been a spending spree on new weapons systems on a scale that the world has not seen since the early years of the Cold War. Scores of new submarines and capital ships; hundreds of front-line fighters and bombers; and hundreds upon hundreds of new cruise and ballistic missiles have been added to the Chinese arsenal. Tellingly, all of this is being done in the face of no new or imminent threat to China. And while China might not be a global military competitor to the United States at the moment, one thing most China-watchers can agree on is that virtually no one would have predicted that China would add this much new military capability in the timeframe that it has.

In addition to these more concrete elements of power, China's rise has also seen a significant increase in the country's sway globally when it comes to diplomatic, political, and even cultural affairs. Ask any foreign ministry official in almost any country about China, and whereas a decade and a half ago he or she would have had little to say about the country other than to mention its ham-handed assertiveness over disputed territories surrounding its borders, today they will talk about a far more confident and sophisticated government whose say in world affairs—be it on the environment, international trade, nuclear proliferation, or energy—is impossible to ignore. And China is no longer a one- or two-note Johnny when it comes to the tools of influence. It has set up "Confucius Institutes" around the globe intended to promote Chinese culture and language and has begun to promote its own model of poverty alleviation as a successful alternative model to that of the so-called "Washington Consensus" of free markets, democracy, and IMF-imposed fiscal guidelines. As David Lampton writes, China "has moved from being a prickly state most comfortable dredging up past humiliations, a nation that eschewed any hint of a desire to play a leadership role, to a more self-assured state."[1]

The concern about China's rise derives from the fact that history suggests rapidly rising powers often bring uncertainty, instability, and competition with them as they begin to assert themselves on the international scene. Naturally enough, such powers wonder why they have to abide by the "rules of the road" in the existing international system when they had little or no voice in establishing those norms. Also, naturally enough, the sheer growth in hard power by the rising nation can't help but make neighboring states and the dominant power in the region concerned about what the future might hold. And, as they react, at least in part by hedging because of their concerns, the rising power will almost certainly read such behavior as an attempt to temper or frustrate its own rightful day in the sun. The result: a potentially combustible mix of ambition, insecurity, and real and perceived grievances.

However, we talk too loosely when we talk about "China's rise." It is not China's rise *per se* that worries Washington, Tokyo, and New Delhi. Rather, it is the rise of the People's Republic of China that causes us concern. As Robert Kagan points out in the chapter that follows, as ambitious as the United States was at the turn of the 20th century, Great Britain, the then-preeminent global power, could tolerate America's rambunctious and assertive policies in this hemisphere and elsewhere more easily because the two countries had more in common politically and culturally than not. That cannot be said about the U.S. and the PRC. The fact that American strategists and policymakers do not lie awake at night thinking about the potential dangers posed by a rising India, for example, just confirms that it is the nature of the polity tied to a country's rise that is as important as the power actually being wielded. The answer to the tongue-in-cheek question posed by *The Economist* as to "Why are there so few takers outside of China for its self-proclaimed doctrine of 'peaceful rise'?" is obvious but obscured by our own hesitancy to state clearly that it is the PRC, not some figurative "China," that is on the rise.

The PRC's governing style has already changed significantly. China under Mao was a ruthless totalitarian dictatorship; today, the PRC is still a one-party state, but one now best described as authoritarian.[2] Presumably, it could change further and do so in a liberal political direction. And there are serious arguments that the PRC's continued economic success will depend on such a change being made and/or being forced on the ruling party by the very success of its own economic policies. Both President Bill Clinton and President George W. Bush developed a U.S. policy toward the PRC that rested on the view that engagement, combined with the country's economic growth, would create a dynamic that would eventually lead to political liberalization. But there is no certainty as to when that might happen and, as with global warming, it matters a great deal whether such an epoch-changing moment is just around the corner or is decades ahead.

Nor is there a consensus that the PRC will in fact make such a turn—or have to.[3] The Chinese Communist Party (CCP) has spent considerable time and effort in examining the collapse of other one-party states, the revolutions that toppled them, and of course the CCP's own near-death experience in 1989 with Tiananmen Square. This is not a leadership or a party that will go gently into the night, or consciously repeat the "mistakes" of the Soviet Union's Gorbachev.[4]

If the Chinese themselves are to be believed, a democratic China is not in the cards. As the government succinctly put it in its most recent white paper on democracy, "Democratic government is the Chinese Communist Party governing on behalf of the people." And, indeed, unlike in the 1980s, when even Communist officials would talk about the merits and prospects for democracy in China, today's discussions are about how to make the one-party state more effective in its governance. Or, as Mark Leonard notes in his book on current intellectual trends in China (*What Does China Think?*), "what has emerged in the place of the liberal democracy that the West predicted [would come to China] is a more sophisticated variant of dictatorship," what he pithily dubs a "deliberative dictatorship."[5] Moreover, the facts on the ground in the PRC are clear enough. The PRC has hardened its stance against political liberalization over the past few years.[6]

In short, the U.S. and the world will likely be dealing with a rising and autocratic PRC for some time to come. "Managing" that rise will be largely out of our hands. By accepting China within the World Trade Organization in 2001, the West gave up the one potentially powerful tool that might have been used to decisively shape PRC behavior—the withholding of trade and economic ties. Of course, the hope was that bringing China into the WTO and other multilateral forums would itself be a significant shaper of Chinese behavior, as China learned to abide by the global rules of the road. And to a degree, that has happened. China's leaders know that their mandate to rule as a one-party state rests in good measure on continuing to deliver the economic goods at home and that, as such, it has a substantial common interest with the United States and other major economies in global economic and financial stability. Yet as anyone working in the U.S. Treasury or the EU Trade Commissioner's office could tell you, China's leaders have not fully embraced a "win-win" approach to economic affairs, and they retain vestiges of a mercantilist approach when it comes to monetary affairs, banking, and natural resources. China's multilateralism appears to be driven as much by simple pragmatism as by having been socialized into accepting liberal internationalist norms. The result has been China taking something akin to a "supermarket" approach to its newfound role as a "responsible stakeholder"—buying what it must, picking up what it wants, and ignoring what it doesn't.

All of which is not surprising. The Chinese believe that, after "one hundred years of humiliation," they are entitled to a bit more leeway in what they do and how they climb out from the hole they have found themselves in. And, indeed, in the absence of elections, and the legitimacy elections provide for rulers, the CCP is under constant pressure to show it is leading the country toward greater and greater prominence. This is exhibited most clearly in the Chinese near-obsession with measuring their country's and other countries' "comprehensive national power."[7] From this point of view, what matters is how the PRC measures up now and tomorrow with other great powers—be it the U.S., Japan, Russia, or India. Although the Chinese have been very careful to look like a cautious power, and in key respects have acted like one, they see the international scene as fundamentally one of competition, not condominium. And this is unlikely to change until and unless the regime changes. It is this China that we will be dealing with for some time to come.

The idea for this book grew out of discussions with my former colleagues at the Project for the New American Century and current colleagues at the American Enterprise Institute for Public Policy Research. Among the great advantages the United States enjoys when it comes to the development of public policy is our system of "think tanks." Left, right, and center, these institutions continue to generate new ideas and analyses that challenge prevailing wisdom or give current policies an intellectual depth that they might not otherwise have. Reflecting their independence, think tanks also foster a continuing debate among themselves that makes our deliberations as a democracy that much healthier. And for those who might work in government after a stint in a think tank, these institutions offer a chance to generate the kind of intellectual capital that the 24/7 life within government depends on but also, sadly, prevents from accruing.

This book is dedicated to my two previous bosses: William Kristol at PNAC and Chris DeMuth at AEI. Both Bill and Chris have shown a remarkable ability to build institutions that are uncommonly effective in driving the policy debates. In addition, they both fostered a climate in which serious ideas were taken seriously, while also making their organizations a congenial place to work. It doesn't get much better.

Others to thank include my various research assistants over the years, but especially Christopher Maletz, Rebecca Weissburg, and Tim Sullivan. All have borne my confusing ways and idiosyncrasies with good humor and unfailing diligence to their work. Thanks, guys.

May 2009

THE RISE OF CHINA

CHAPTER ONE

AMBITION AND ANXIETY

America's Competition with China

Robert Kagan

I f ambition is a sin, then all great powers in history have been sinners. Throughout recorded history, when powerful peoples, city-states, and nations have arisen, they have often found themselves in a struggle to shape the contours of their world. These historical struggles are never about power alone, territory, or even physical security. The great struggles of history have also been about definitions of morality and justice, about competing visions of the role of the individual and society, about tradition and change, about images and interpretations of the divine.

The struggle between China and the United States that will dominate the 21st century is about both power and belief. Two rising, ambitious powers are contesting for leadership in East Asia. As the world's strongest democracy and the world's strongest autocracy, however, they are also engaged in a contest about ideas, about definitions of justice, morality, and legitimacy, about order and liberalism.

Today, neither China nor the United States wants war, and wise statesmanship on both sides may avoid it for years and even decades to come, perhaps long enough for circumstances to change and the confrontation to dissipate. Neither Americans nor Chinese should delude themselves, however. All the classic conditions for conflict are already in place; they merely await the right sequence of events to provide a spark. Nor is this Sino-American confrontation a product of misunderstandings or errors that just need to be cleared up. It is not an anomaly. It is normal, the unavoidable consequence of two powerful nations with clashing ambitions and colliding worldviews, and also with much in common.

It is on the subject of power that America and China have the most in common. Both seek power and believe power is necessary to defend and promote their interests and beliefs. Both deny this, of course, because the 21st-century world recoils at discussions of power. Yet the United States spent more on its military than the next dozen powers combined even before September 11, 2001. Nor has it been shy about using it, with ten military interventions in the past two decades alone. In the same two decades, China has been increasing military spending by more than ten percent per year. It will soon spend as much on defense as all the nations of the European Union combined.

Power changes nations. It expands their wants and desires, increases their sense of entitlement, their need for deference and respect. It also makes them more ambitious. It lessens their tolerance to obstacles, their willingness to take no for an answer.

This has certainly been true of the United States throughout its history. Indeed, if Americans want to understand Chinese power and ambition today, they could start by looking in the mirror. They could look back at the 19th century, when their own increasingly powerful nation, like China today, began knocking at the door of an existing international system in which it had until then played but a small part.

After the Civil War, Americans were more secure than at any time in their history. They faced no threat of invasion and were rapidly becoming one of the richest nations on earth. Their expanding domestic market attracted vast amounts of foreign investment. The European empires that once surrounded the United States on all sides were retreating from the Western Hemisphere, effectively ceding it to American hegemony. And no sooner had Americans acquired this unparalleled security and regional dominance than, starting in the early 1880s, they began a peacetime naval buildup and the creation of a new battleship fleet that within two decades made America one of the top naval powers in the world.

The buildup was not a defensive reaction to foreign threats, which were practically nonexistent. It was the product of expanding ambitions. American presidents talked about becoming "the arbiter" of the Pacific, "the controller of its commerce," a "power to be reckoned with."[1]

For all their security and power, many Americans in the 1890s felt challenged, constrained, even suffocated by other powers both great and not great. They imagined Great Britain and other European powers were standing in their way, denying them what was rightfully theirs. They felt a hostile world closing in and building barriers around them. But it was they who were pushing out into the world.[2] Power produced ambition, and ambition in turn produced anxiety.

Power, Interest, and Ambition

China's story has not been so different. Sixty years ago, China was on its back: torn by domestic conflict, oppressed by foreign powers, vulnerable, poor, and isolated. Today, as Mao put it, China has "stood up." Since the reforms begun by Deng Xiaoping in the late 1970s, its economy has grown more rapidly than any in history. It is a rising geopolitical giant, secure within its borders, its economy racing to become the largest in the world, its military power steadily growing, and its political influence expanding apace. Few nations in history have ever moved further and faster from weakness to strength, from vulnerability to security.

So is China becoming satisfied? It has never been richer, and it has never been safer. In the first two decades after 1949, it faced constant war or the threat of war—in Korea, with Nationalist Taiwan, and with India. By the late 1960s, it had antagonized both superpowers, and when the Soviet Union put a million men on China's frontier in 1969, the Chinese did not have a friend in the world to help them. Then came rapprochement with the United States, which provided security against the Soviet threat and ended China's international isolation. Over the next three decades, China masterfully regained sovereign control over most of the territories lost in the 19th century. By the end of the Cold War, it faced no serious threat of attack from any direction. By the dawn of the 21st century, it faced "no tangible or immediate external military threat" and was stronger than at any time in the modern era.[3]

So how did China respond to this unprecedented power and security? It responded predictably. It responded by wanting more.

Thucydides wrote that nations are driven by three concerns: interest, honor, and fear. China is no exception. The irony for American policymakers today is that China's economic liberalization and economic expansion have produced the money for China's military expansion. For most of the past two decades, and even today, American and European observers have assumed that China's economic growth and modernization would somehow moderate, tame, and liberalize Chinese behavior both at home and abroad.

It worked, but not entirely the way American policymakers imagined. The Chinese have developed an interest in the well-being of the global economy, and particularly of the American economy, on which China relies for its life's blood. But there is another side to China's Americanization. Being a great commercial nation does not

4

mean being a pacific nation. On the contrary. America, as the world's greatest commercial power, also made itself the world's strongest military power.

The Chinese have the same practical reasons that motivated Americans. Over recent decades, as their economy has been transformed and they have become deeply enmeshed in the international liberal economic order, they, too, have gained a new set of far-flung economic interests, from Asia to Africa to the Middle East and Latin America. And like great capitalist nations of the past, the Chinese increasingly believe they need to do what they can to guarantee access to these markets, energy resources, and raw materials.

There has been a corresponding shift in Chinese military strategy. The Chinese used to count on their massive population to provide a massive army capable of defeating any invasion. But China no longer fears invasion. Its expanding interests, and changing technologies of warfare, have redirected its attention outward. Officials began talking of extending China's strategic frontiers progressively outward to what they called the three "island chains." The first, running from Japan to Taiwan to the Philippines, would constitute China's naval defense perimeter by 2010. By 2025, China would establish a wider perimeter running from Sakhalin to the islands of the Southwest Pacific. The "third island chain," running from the Aleutian Islands off Alaska to the Antarctic, "was to be the goal by 2050."[4] The Chinese navy has a long way to go before being able to accomplish the most ambitious of these objectives. But the will and the desire are there.

There is more to the Chinese buildup than security and economics. For the Chinese, as for all rising powers, there is also a matter of honor and status, a desire for greatness and recognition. The Chinese people and their leaders have a new confidence, a new pride, and a not unreasonable feeling that the future belongs to them. This competitive nationalism is neither unusual nor unique to the Chinese. A booming economy shaped Americans' self-perceptions in the late 1890s. It shaped Japanese self-perceptions in the 1980s, and it shapes India's self-perceptions today. Russia's new oil and gas wealth has also revived Russian ambitions. And, of course, many nations have at some time in their history harbored ambitions for greatness on the world stage.

Today, it is China's turn to have such pretensions and aspirations. For over a millennium, China was the dominant power in Asia, the only advanced civilization in a world of barbarians. Then for about a century, from the 1840s to the 1940s, the Chinese found themselves weak, vulnerable, and humiliatingly "thrown out to the margins" of a suddenly Eurocentric world.[5] It was a terrible aberration, in the Chinese view. Today, many Chinese believe that their nation's ancient centrality, appropriately adjusted for the times and circumstances, can, should, and will be recaptured.[6]

Today, Chinese greatness is measured by the respect their nation is accorded by others, by China's new weight in international economic councils, by the solicitousness of other nations and of the world's most powerful multinational corporations. Pride in China's growing international status has become one of the great sources of legitimacy of the ruling oligarchy of the Chinese Communist Party. As one Chinese diplomat described his own excitement at this transformation of China's relationship with the great powers of the world, "Today it is our turn to speak and their turn to listen."[7]

Pride, honor, status, and the desire for independence all help explain why the Chinese in recent years have wanted to play a larger role defending their economic interests overseas. For decades, China, like most other nations in the world, has allowed the American navy to be the great protector of its interests abroad, patrolling the sea lanes, guarding the oil supplies, insuring the international free flow of commerce with its battleships and aircraft carriers. American scholars call this one of the "public goods" the United States provides to the world.

From the Chinese perspective, however, it is has never been an unmitigated good. It is one thing for Japan and Europe to trust their lives to the American navy, but it is another thing entirely for China. As a commentary in the official *Liberation Army Daily* explained, "As China's comprehensive strength is incrementally mounting and her status keeps on going up in international affairs, it is a matter of great importance to strive to construct a military force that is commensurate with China's status and up to the job of defending the interests of China's development, so as to entrench China's international status."[8] The purpose of China's military modernization is not only to deter attack and protect vital interests but also to "enable China to play the role of an authentic great power."[9]

This equation of military strength with international standing and respectability may be troubling to postmodern sensibilities. In Europe, and even, oddly, in the United States, many believe that military power and nationalism are a deadly combination that should be relegated to the past. Behind these very postmodern expressions of disapproval, of course, are some very traditional concerns. Americans are the predominant power and naturally don't want to be challenged. Europeans had great power, lost it, and now claim that military power no longer matters. The last thing they want to see is the rise of another great power that believes it does.

But history is hard to escape. Are the Chinese alone expected to forego this traditional path of rising powers, the path of increasing military as well as economic and political power?

A Different Power?

There are those who insist that China is different. They argue, in the words of the Chinese scholar Zheng Bijian, that China will "transcend the traditional ways for great powers to emerge, as well as the Cold War mentality that defined international relations along ideological lines. . . . Instead, China will transcend ideological differences to strive for peace, development, and cooperation with all countries of the world."[10] It's a sentiment worthy of a Hallmark card, but is it possible?

The Chinese leadership today would also like to foster this image. They know that their growing economic, political, and military strength is raising international concerns, and they are eager to avoid the fate of Germany and Japan and the Soviet Union, each of which inspired fear and produced coalitions of powerful nations against them. In the early 1990s, Deng created a set of guidelines for Chinese foreign policy that subsequent leaders have done their best to follow: "Observe calmly; secure our position; cope with affairs calmly; hide our capacities and bide our time; be good at maintaining a low profile; and never claim leadership." When Zheng Bijian wrote his famous essay, it was soothingly entitled "China's Peaceful Rise." But government officials worried that it wasn't soothing enough, that even the word "rise" was too frightening. They changed the phrase to "China's Peaceful Development." The effort displayed remarkable self-awareness.

But China's emergence as a traditional great power cannot be ignored or wished away. It is not being ignored in its own neighborhood. Nations like Japan and Australia now routinely express concern about the growth of Chinese military power, wonder about its intentions, and seek to strengthen their alliances with the United States.

And if national honor for the Chinese requires being treated as roughly an equal by the world's other great powers, in their own neighborhood of East Asia the Chinese aspire to more than equality. Insofar as the Chinese people have a sense of "manifest destiny," its most vivid, most practicable, and most immediate expression is the desire to restore their ancient centrality within the region that extends from the Korean peninsula and Japan in Northeast Asia to the nations of Southeast Asia and the archipelagoes of the Philippines, Indonesia, and Malaysia.

One reason people and nations want power is to right past wrongs. China's return to regional primacy is also a necessary part of rectifying past injustices. For the Chinese there has been no greater injustice than the suffering inflicted by Japan, not only in the 1930s and '40s but going back to the late 19th century, when Japan first defeated China militarily and imposed a humiliating peace settlement. The Chinese certainly expect growing power will restore justice to their relations with the Japanese.

Justice does not mean equality. For more than a thousand years, the Chinese looked down on the Japanese as an inferior race within the Chinese culture. They either treated Japan "benevolently as a student or younger brother" or malevolently as a nation of "pirates," but viewed from China's perspective, Chinese superiority and Japanese inferiority were part of the natural order of things.[11] In Confucian terms, such hierarchical relationships make for "harmonious" relations.[12]

This ideal relationship was turned upside down at the end of the 19th century, when a rising, westernizing Japan thrashed China in the war of 1895. As one angry Chinese writer put it in a 1997 diatribe, "China lost to her 'student.'"[13] Chinese scholars call the 1895 Treaty of Shimonoseki the "greatest humiliation" in China's history.[14] China ceded control over Korea and Taiwan to Japan and was effectively stripped of all pretenses of national power.

Many argue that the anti-Japanese sentiment in China is fanned by Beijing. Perhaps, but Chinese leaders don't have to work very hard to manufacture popular anger at Japan. The Chinese national anthem, like the American national anthem, was composed during a war. But Americans scarcely remember the War of 1812, let alone why they fought it. When the Chinese people sing, "Arise, Ye who refuse to be slaves! With our very flesh and blood, Let us build our new Great Wall! . . . Arise! Arise! Arise!"—they are singing about a Japanese invasion that elderly Chinese can still recall. "Millions of hearts with one mind. . . . Everybody must roar his defiance!"

China has tried to establish its predominant influence not by power alone. Like the United States in the Western Hemisphere, China's main strength has been its economy. It has deepened economic ties with the nations of East Asia and the Pacific, proposed Asian free-trade zones, and even been willing to accept disadvantageous terms, in keeping with the ancient tributary principle of "give more, take less."[15] It has pursued confident and capable diplomacy, settling old border disputes with neighboring countries, participating in established regional international institutions, and also helping to found new ones.

China's use of diplomacy and economics does not distinguish it from traditional rising and hegemonic powers. In the 19th century, the United States took part in regional conferences, and it designed and created new multilateral institutions to preserve peace and order in the hemisphere. But it was an American peace and an American order. American "good neighbor" policies only reinforced America's role as the self-appointed policeman of the neighborhood.

In the same way, China has sought to strengthen multilateral organizations in East Asia in recent years, such as the Association of Southeast Asian Nations (ASEAN), whose members include Thailand, the Philippines, Cambodia, Myanmar, Brunei, Singapore, Laos, Indonesia, Vietnam, and Malaysia; and it has helped build new institutions, such as the Shanghai Cooperation Organization (SCO), which groups China with Kazakhstan, Kyrgyzstan, Tajikistan, Uzbekistan, and Russia. It has promoted the East Asia Summit, an annual meeting of the ASEAN nations plus China, Korea, and Japan.

This is not a budding European Union in Asia. In the EU, several great powers as well as many smaller powers come to the table as relative equals. Their militaries no longer even have plans on the shelf for possible wars against each other. In East Asia, the discussions are more lopsided, with many small powers and one large power (or in the case of the SCO, one-and-a-half.) They are not among equals, and the military imbalance hovers over the room. China's involvement in East Asian diplomatic fora is less an attempt to recreate the European Union than to recreate the Organization of American States. Lilliputians can pretend to tie Gulliver down with threads, but Gulliver can stand up when he wants to.

An Anxious Power

If the Chinese search for greater "comprehensive national power" is partly driven by the Thucydidean triad of honor, interest, and fear, what is it that the Chinese fear? They fear what all rising powers fear: that they will be denied. The Chinese do feel threatened, but not by invasion. What they fear is obstruction. They worry that an American-led world will try to stop them from fulfilling their ambitions and their destiny. And the leaders of China have their own special fear, that the denial of Chinese ambitions abroad could ultimately undermine their ability to rule at home. So the cycle continues: Chinese power has produced ambition, and ambition in turn has produced anxiety.

This helps explain the apparent paradox that has puzzled many foreign observers of China's behavior over the past decade. Although stronger and more secure than ever, China has often acted in a "highly provocative manner," as if it were "faced with a threat greater than ever before."[16]

This is not as paradoxical as it seems. China has progressed from a nation seeking only to survive to a nation seeking more than survival. The purpose of Chinese power today and in the future is not only to defend against attack, but "to prevent foreseeable international roadblocks on the path to greatness that Beijing plans to follow."[17] But that is a daunting task. The more China seeks to shape its world, the more others may resist.

In the Chinese case, this resistance is not an optical illusion. The roadblocks they perceive are real. Within the East Asian region there is the problem of Japan, and there is the problem of Taiwan. And behind both of these lies the biggest problem of all, the United States.

Americans, typically, don't regard themselves as a threat to China. The official policy of the United States, spanning several recent administrations, has been one of cooperation and engagement. Privately, American officials also acknowledge an element of "hedging" in the strategy: a kind of preventive military and alliance posture that, like an automobile airbag, can be inflated upon impact. But Americans deny, with varying degrees of sincerity, that they want to contain China's rise. They see their own actions as purely defensive and reactive. China may be ambitious, but the United States is a status quo power, or so Americans believe.

The United States is like a person on a train who imagines that only the countryside is moving. Since the start of the 20th century, the United States has been the world's leading agent of change, perhaps the most revolutionary nation in history, constantly shaping and reshaping the world around it, in pursuit of its interests and ideals. Yet Americans imagine, and have always imagined, that they are only reacting to the changing world around them.

But the United States has never been a status quo power, not in the world, and not in East Asia.

America's deep interest in East Asia goes back to the 18th century, when the young nation hoped to finance its emergence from the shadow of British power by opening trade with the East. From the beginning, many Americans saw East Asia, and especially China, as a place of great riches and appalling backwardness. In characteristic Anglo-Saxon fashion, they hoped both to prosper and to help. At first tentative in its interventions in the region, operating behind the shield of British naval power, over the course of the 19th century the United States insisted on becoming an Asian power on its own. It planted its flag in the region, with a colony in the Philippines, influential missionary establishments in China and Korea, numerous treaties of trade and friendship signed by its hyperactive diplomats, and a growing American naval presence. By the dawn of the 20th century, American military power was a significant part of the East Asian equation. American naval vessels patrolled Asian waters. In 1900, the United States dispatched several thousand marines to China during the Boxer Rebellion. It also arrogated to itself the role of protector of China's territorial integrity against the acquisitive imperialism of Russia and the European powers—something that would have seemed absurd even two decades before and was in fact far too ambitious for America's limited resources at the time.

The first four decades of the 20th century gradually but brutally exposed the vast gap between American ambitions in East Asia and American means and will to back them up. The challenge to American influence then was not Russia or Europe but Japan, which had grand ambitions of its own to be the predominant East Asian power. When Japan invaded Manchuria and began a course of conquest in China in the 1930s, the United States, practically alone among the great powers, registered protests and imposed sanctions. In the 1930s, the United States took escalating steps against Japan that were both too feeble to stop its conquest of China and yet strong enough to convince the Japanese that the United States was an obstacle to their ambitions in East Asia. That realization eventually led to the attack on the American fleet at Pearl Harbor.

The Japanese attack, though tactically successful, failed in its larger strategic purpose of convincing the Americans to pull back from East Asia. Instead of tempering American ambitions, Pearl Harbor drove Americans to expand them (not unlike the more recent effect of the September 11 attacks). Even as they fought, American leaders decided that the United States would not leave East Asia at all after the war but would establish itself permanently as the predominant power in the region.

American strategic goals in 1945 were not so dissimilar from Chinese strategic ambitions today. The United States "redefined the U.S. strategic perimeter and insisted on preserving hegemony over the Pacific and Atlantic oceans." Americans traced an arc from Indonesia to the Philippines to Taiwan and Japan, their own "island chain," and military officials recommended establishing a string of bases in East Asia. They wanted to plan ahead, "not for ten years but 50–100 years ahead." During the Cold War, those bases provided the launching point for massive American interventions in both Northeast and Southeast Asia, in Korea and Vietnam, two countries bordering on China. Today, more than sixty years later, many of those bases remain and serve roughly the same function as originally intended, only now against a different potential adversary.[18]

The rise of China in East Asia in the past two decades has challenged but not dislodged American hegemony. Instead of accepting a new balance of power in the region, the United States since the 1990s has responded to growing Chinese power by broadening and deepening its military relationship with Japan, strengthening its strategic relationship with Taiwan, maintaining forces in South Korea, deepening military cooperation with the Philippines, Indonesia, Australia, and other Southeast Asian nations, and also with Pakistan and Afghanistan, all as part of the fight against terrorism. It has reached out to India, sanctioning its nuclear weapons program in the interest of closer strategic ties. Americans would deny that any of this constitutes a new strategy of containment aimed at China, much less an effort to preserve American hegemony. But the Chinese see it as both. Here is how China's current premier, Hu Jintao, describes the course of an American foreign policy that Americans themselves see as merely reactive:

> [The United States has] strengthened its military deployments in the Asia-Pacific region, strengthened the U.S.-Japan military alliance, strengthened strategic cooperation with India, improved relations with Vietnam, inveigled Pakistan, established a pro-American government in Afghanistan, increased arms sales to Taiwan, and so on. They have extended outposts and placed pressure points from the east, south, and west.[19]

For the Chinese, there was nothing unusual about this, either. "Hegemony and power politics are a long term historical phenomenon in international politics," Chinese strategic thinkers pointed out.[20] America was only acting "rationally and coherently in pursuit of the singular goal of extending its hegemonic influence throughout the world,"[21] and the fall of the Soviet Union had naturally increased America's "lust for leading the world and its tendency of expansionism."[22] As Wen Jiabao has expressed the consensus view of the Chinese leadership, "The United States is trying to preserve its status as the world's sole superpower, and will not allow any country the chance to pose a challenge to it."[23]

The New Clash of Old Ideologies

Competition between the United States and China is not the only possible scenario, however. One can imagine a situation in which a gradual decline in American power and influence in East Asia produced not war but a *Pax Sinica*. Great powers, and even superpowers, have given way to rising regional powers in the past, even to former rivals. Great Britain withdrew from the Western Hemisphere at the end of the 19th century and ceded the region to a rather belligerent United States.[24] More recently, the United States has been gradually ceding its once-dominant position in Europe to the leadership of the European Union.

Would the United States pursue a similar course in East Asia? It is unlikely. The reason is not only that Americans would fear instability, insecurity, a loss of trade and access to resources, or damage to other American material interests. After all, a *Pax Sinica* might well provide secure access to trade and resources, and even a stable peace. What makes the situation in East Asia different is something less tangible but perhaps more powerful. It is the conflicting ideologies of the United States and China. Great Britain could cede the Western Hemisphere to the United States in part because it was a fellow liberal democracy, and they shared common social values and political and economic principles. At a time when the British people faced a growing challenge from Germany and Russia, whose political and cultural values they did not share, they trusted the American democracy not to turn its growing power and influence against them. Similarly, the United States can reduce its role in Europe because the continent has become, as Americans like to say, "whole and free." Even though the United States fought two horrific wars against European powers in the past century, Americans cannot really imagine Europe turning its power against them again. In American eyes, the ideological transformation of Europe has been decisive.

In East Asia, the situation is different. There is a clash not only of competitive powers, but also of competitive political systems. Because China is not a democracy, and its leaders insist they have no intention of making it one, Americans, quite simply, don't trust it. Chinese leaders have their own fears and suspicions. They recognize America's ideological hostility. Because they are not a democracy, they fear that a persistent and growing American liberal hegemony in East Asia, with its ring of democratic states on China's periphery, will eventually undermine their legitimacy at home. Indeed, the Chinese may have an even clearer sense than most Americans about what a large role ideology plays in shaping the relationship between the two powers.

Some question whether today's Chinese leaders have an ideology. They are not democrats, certainly, but they no longer seem to be committed communists either. But liberalism and communism are not the only ideologies the world has ever known. Chinese leaders clearly do have a set of beliefs that guides them in both domestic and foreign policy. They believe China's economic growth requires order, and order can only come from above, from the strong hand of government. They believe China is simply too big and too diverse to be run by the people. They believe that a strong government is both good and necessary for China, that it is preferable to the weakness and vacillation of democracy, which they believe would produce chaos and shatter the nation. The Chinese leaders are autocrats, and they believe autocracy is in the people's interest.

China's foreign policy naturally reflects the autocratic character of its government. In the age of monarchy, foreign policy served the interests of the monarchy. In the age of religious conflict, it served the interests of the church. In the modern era, democracies have pursued foreign policies to make the world safe for democracy. And autocracies pursue foreign policies aimed at making the world safe for autocracy. Today, the competition between them, along with the struggle of radical Islamists to make the world safe for their vision of Islamic theocracy, has become a defining feature of the international scene. China may no longer be communist, but it does have an ideology, and a foreign policy to protect it.

And there is much to protect it from. Americans view the world through the lens of their own brand of liberalism, often blurring distinctions between the ideological and the strategic. Since the early days of the republic, they have often judged other nations as good or bad, friendly or hostile, largely by the nature of their governments. In this liberal worldview, there is a simple explanation for the connection between a nation's polity and its foreign policy. Governments not founded on the consent of the governed are by nature illegitimate, by liberal logic. They are unstable and insecure. They live in constant fear of their own people, and they rely on force to keep themselves in power. Naturally, they rely on force in dealing with the world, too. They compensate for their illegitimacy at home with aggressive and belligerent behavior abroad, especially toward liberal, democratic governments, whom they fear the most.

What distinguishes most Americans from other democracies, especially in Europe, is that Americans more often believe they have the power, the right, and at times even the obligation to act on this liberal principle, to effect change in other countries, to transform tyrannies in order to make the world safer for democracies. If, as Americans believed, Nazi Germany and Imperial Japan were dangerous and aggressive because they were governed by fascist dictators or militaristic emperors, then to build an enduring peace after World War II required removing the cause of the danger and turning them into democracies. If the Soviet Union was aggressive abroad because it was a brutal tyranny at home, as observers from George F. Kennan onward have asserted, then the best strategy was to contain it from without and encourage change from within. If and when the Soviet Union opened up its system, most Americans believed, it would no longer be a threat.

The end of the Cold War seemed to vindicate Americans' faith in liberalism. The apparent triumph of this liberal worldview, coupled with America's rise to become the world's only superpower, gave the United States an almost unbounded confidence in the link between the ideology and strategy. It scarcely occurred to most Americans that what seemed indisputably good to them might not seem so to those who did not share their worldview.

The events of 1989 and the years that followed did not appear indisputably good to the Chinese leadership. Indeed, to comprehend the ideological conflict between the United States and China, one only has to understand how the end of the Cold War looked from Beijing's perspective.

For Americans and Europeans, 1989 was a year of miracles. For the Chinese Communist Party it was a year of disasters, the year of Tiananmen Square, in which an uprising of students and workers came close to threatening the party's control of the nation and forced it to call out the army to restore order, in full view of the entire world.

It was the year in which the international liberal community led by the United States turned on China with a rare unity, imposing economic sanctions and an even more painful diplomatic isolation. It was the year China's leaders nearly lost everything.

To the democratic world, the violence in Tiananmen Square was an unexpected deviation from what had seemed China's steady, liberalizing path throughout the 1980s. It violated the whole post-Cold War liberal paradigm. The Chinese leadership, however, did not want to be on the road to democracy, which had almost led them off a cliff. Gorbachev to them was no hero; he was the very model of what not to do. He forgot that his rule depended ultimately not on the will of the people but on the power of the state. When he dissipated that power, the Chinese leadership believed, he lost everything, not only his own power and his party's but also his capacity to reform and strengthen his nation. The ensuing chaos of the Yeltsin years vindicated the view that without a strong hand, the mob and the kleptocracy would rule and the people would suffer.

If the events of 1989 introduced Chinese leaders to the new realities of the post-Cold War era, the collapse of Soviet power, coupled with the events in Tiananmen Square, also transformed American attitudes toward China. For the better part of two decades, from the 1970s to the mid-1980s, the United States had mostly submerged its ideological distaste for the Chinese government in the interest of strategic partnership against the Soviets. Then in 1989, China suddenly became more distasteful, just as American fear of the Soviets vanished. The Chinese could see that lurking behind the American condemnation of their behavior in June 1989 was a new strategic calculation. The United States, having done away with one adversary, was training its sights on the next potential threat. Americans had made such sharp strategic pivots before. The Soviet Union led by "Uncle Joe" Stalin had been a far more vital ally during World War II than China ever was during the Cold War. Yet in a matter of months after their common foe, Nazi Germany, had been vanquished, the Americans began to see the Soviets as their next big problem. From the Chinese perspective, 1989 was their 1945.

The United States after 1989 solidified its place as the leader of a clique of advanced democracies sharing roughly similar ideological perspectives on most important matters. Liberalism became the dominant worldview, sustained by an "international hierarchy dominated by the United States and its democratic allies," a "U.S.-centered great power group." In this global club, the Chinese were an "outlier," and therefore a target.[25]

Today, China itself is more powerful, less isolated, more influential, and more accepted by the liberal clique than it was at the beginning of the post-Cold War era. But the structural realities have not changed that much since 1989. The United States remains dominant, despite the Iraq War. Even the damage done to transatlantic relations has not really broken up the liberal "in-group" as much as the Chinese hoped it might.

Seen from Beijing, the years since the fall of the Berlin Wall have provided a disturbing picture of what a sole remaining superpower can do with its power and influence. Since 1989, the United States has toppled governments in Panama and Haiti, bombed Serbia twice, and Afghanistan and Sudan once, not to mention the three interventions against Iraq under Bush, Clinton, and Bush. But even more than that, it has used its power to shape the world in its liberal image. The United States, Chinese observers argue, is not like past empires. Its aim has not been to conquer territory but to conquer minds, to transform political systems, to acquire "dominance over the thinking and ideology of the world."[26] By promoting economic "liberalization" and political "democratization," it hopes to achieve the "global popularization of the American political system and American values."[27]

That is how Chinese analysts and their government counterparts viewed the "humanitarian" interventions of the 1990s, in Haiti, Somalia, Bosnia, and Kosovo. That is how they interpreted the first Bush administration's New World Order, the Clinton administration's policy of "democratic enlargement," and the second Bush administration's "freedom doctrine." This entire "ideological crusade," with its "interventionist emphasis on human rights," has been a new and potent strategy of global domination.[28] From 2003 to 2005 the transatlantic democracies cheered on the "color revolutions" in Georgia, Ukraine, Kyrgyzstan, and Lebanon, where opposition movements toppled entrenched autocracies through elections; the Chinese did not cheer. What Americans and Europeans see as their own disinterested humanitarianism, the Chinese see as hegemonism. Where Americans and Europeans see the triumph of reason, the Chinese see only the triumph of power.

American policymakers say they want China to integrate itself into the international liberal order, but the Chinese are understandably wary. Will that liberal order protect the Chinese leadership's interests, or is it more likely to undermine them over time? From the Chinese point of view, the trends in the international order have not been encouraging. Since the end of the Cold War, the dominant transatlantic democracies have been trying to modify traditional international law and practices to permit intervention in the internal affairs of nations. They have been devising new legal principles— "limited sovereignty," the "responsibility to protect"—all with the same aim: to legitimize international intervention against tyrants who either abuse their own people or fail to protect them from humanitarian disaster. In this new vision of international law, nations can forfeit their right to sovereignty if the "international community" judges them to be massively violating the rights of their people.

The Europeans have been complicit in promoting this new vision of world order. The European Union, after all, is an institution founded on the principle of diminished national sovereignty, devoted to meddling and interfering in the internal affairs of its members, so much so that even they occasionally balk at the intrusions. With their more lax attitude toward sovereignty, and their historical ties to Africa, Europeans are even more angered than Americans by China's refusal to use its increasing economic influence against dictators in Zimbabwe, Sudan, and elsewhere—as if it could possibly be in the interest of one autocrat to help liberal nations undermine the power of another autocrat. Unfortunately for the Chinese, this is one area where there is no great transatlantic divide. The Europeans are

America's enablers in breaking down the barriers of national sovereignty of illiberal states. And although the Americans and Europeans advancing these new notions of limited sovereignty do not consciously aim them at China, the Chinese leadership understandably worries about a future in which international law allows liberal governments to intervene wherever and whenever their collective liberal consciences move them.

That is not the kind of international order Chinese leaders want. They prefer to restore the old international order that is embodied in the UN Charter and rests on three centuries of international legal principle, in which national sovereignty was held sacred and inviolable (at least in theory). Collective action against individual states was permissible only in response to unprovoked acts of aggression and only after authorization by the UN Security Council, on which China wields a veto. It is a great irony of history that the Chinese Communist Party, which once stood for world revolution and did not believe in national sovereignty at all, has now become the leading apostle and defender of the old Westphalian system, the invention of the 17th-century European autocracies for the defense of autocracy, in which inviolable national sovereignty was supposed to reign supreme above all other values.[29]

The Chinese can see no principled justification for this great shift. It can only be part of the overall ideological and strategic struggle waged by the United States. As the strategic thinker Yan Xuetong puts it, the Americans want to create "an institutionalized system of hegemony" by "establishing international norms" in accordance with American principles of behavior. Once these norms are "accepted by a majority of countries," then American hegemony becomes "legitimized."[30] As Chinese officials asked at the time of Tiananmen Square, and have continued to ask ever since, "What right does the U.S. government have to make irresponsible remarks about and flagrantly interfere in China's internal affairs?"[31]

What right, indeed? To those who share the liberal worldview, the right comes from the liberal creed itself, that all men are created equal and have certain inalienable rights that must not be abridged by governments, and that governments derive their power and legitimacy only from the consent of the governed. But to the Chinese and others who don't share this view, the United States and its democratic allies succeed in imposing their views on others only because they are powerful enough to do so. It is not a case of right makes might, as Americans and Europeans like to claim, but of might makes right. From the Chinese view, what is to stop the United States and its democratic allies from interfering again if the Chinese government finds itself challenged as it was in 1989?

Such a prospect is not only likely but practically certain. The United States has never stopped seeking change in China's political system. Although the days of economic sanctions have passed and China is a member of the World Trade Organization and an invitee to G 8 summits, the declared goals of American policy have not changed since 1989. The United States wants to steer China in what Americans regard as a beneficial direction, smoothing and hastening its integration into the existing international order both economically and politically, enmeshing it in international economic agreements, taking advantage of the fact that economic development has been China's overriding priority to nudge China in a more liberal direction politically. In the meantime it strengthens American alliances, reassures China's democratic neighbors, and creates sufficient American military, economic, and political strength in East Asia to prevent China from achieving its regional ambitions. Contain and transform, or, in the more polite phrases of diplomacy, "hedge" and engage. Given its beliefs and its history, it is hard to imagine the United States pursuing any other kind of policy toward China.

Conclusion

China's autocratic rulers know they cannot count on the existing international order to protect them from these liberalizing forces. They cannot count on other nations to join them in checking American power. Even if Europeans grumble about American hegemonism, they are themselves part of the structure of global liberal hegemony. Chinese leaders can only count on themselves.

In the end, they must either conform or resist. Conforming means their demise. At best, it means going the way of Gorbachev. At worst, it means going the way of Ceausescu. They must somehow make the world safe, if not for autocracy, then at least for their own continued rule. The world must be convinced to accommodate not only a rising China but an autocratic China. And it is only likely to do so if it has no choice. Power, both economic and military, will have to compensate for the disadvantage of being an autocracy in a liberal age. The Chinese don't have the luxury of pretending, as the postmodern world would like them to pretend, that power is not relevant to their future survival.

CHAPTER TWO

CHINA'S GRAND STRATEGY

The Quest for Comprehensive National
Power and Its Consequences

Ashley J. Tellis

W hen Deng Xiaoping unleashed market reforms in 1978, neither he nor his successors could have imagined how revolutionary those decisions would turn out to be for China's geopolitical
fortunes. Freed from cataclysmic Maoist political upheavals and a
controlled Soviet-style economy, China would over the next three decades experience, in the words of *The Economist*, "the most dynamic
burst of wealth creation in human history."[1] Thanks to Deng's initiative, China's economic performance would eclipse even the improvements brought about by the pre-reform Communist state after

the disastrous past century of Qing rule: agricultural productivity increased as the size of production units decreased dramatically; a huge expansion of small-scale industry, especially in rural areas, contributed to increased efficiency of capital use and significant increases in productivity growth; manufacturing and exports increased stupendously, with China's share of world exports increasing from less than 1 percent in 1978 to more than 8 percent in 2006; the annual inflow of foreign direct investment, which was insignificant at the beginning of the reform period, skyrocketed, now standing in excess of $60 billion; and while Beijing's external indebtedness remains extraordinarily low, its accumulated foreign exchange reserves now consist, stratospherically, of more than $1.5 trillion.

The past thirty years of economic reform, which begat a retrenchment of state controls, a permissive new environment for rural enterprises and private businesses, a dramatic increase in industrial production and export performance, and new investments in education and human capital formation, have thus turned out to be a spectacular success. This is evident from the fact that throughout this period China chalked up average real growth in excess of 9 percent annually, with growth rates sometimes touching 13 and 14 percent in peak years. Not surprisingly, per capita income in China rose by more than 6 percent every year from 1978 to 2003—much faster than any other Asian country, very much better than the 1.8 percent per year in Western Europe and the United States, and four times as fast as the world average. This has made the Chinese economy—when measured by purchasing power parity methods—the second largest in the world. If current trends hold, China could at some point overtake the United States to become the world's largest economy, as it was at least from the 10th to the 15th century. This achievement, if and when it comes about, would enable Beijing to recover the geopolitical preeminence it last enjoyed under the Ming Dynasty and, depending on how successfully China translates its economic strength into broad development, could enable it to mount serious political challenges to the United States both in Asia and in the larger international system.

The Quest for Comprehensive National Power in a Historical Context

Right from the beginning of the reform period, when Deng launched the "four modernizations" intended to transform China's agriculture, industry, science and technology, and military at the Third Plenum of the 11th Central Committee in December 1978, the principal objective of China's grand strategy has been the accumulation of "comprehensive national power." Although this phrase itself was not formally articulated until the 1980s—and, when articulated, referred principally to specific Chinese quantitative efforts to assess the relative power of states—the underlying notion of developing national capabilities in an all-encompassing fashion to include the material, institutional, and ideational elements of power was clearly inherent in Deng's vision. As John Garver aptly summarized it, "the broad purpose of China's Deng-inspired drive for modernization [was] to make China rich and powerful, thereby restoring it to the position of high international influence and status that it enjoyed throughout most of the several millennia of its existence."[2]

That China should entertain notions of recovering greatness, and more specifically its primacy in the Asian and global systems, ought not to be surprising given that China has long possessed all the attributes associated with great powers in international politics: huge territory, vast resources, large population, and significant military capabilities. Until the advent of the modern era, China was in fact one of the globe's most powerful political entities: it consisted of an impressive centrally-administered bureaucratic state controlling large territory; it possessed the world's largest economy; it maintained a unique sphere of influence, if not control, that spanned much of East and Southeast Asia, with significant reach into Central Asia as well; and it deployed large and proficient military forces that were used, as appropriate and with requisite vigor, to preserve domestic order and support its external interests along a vast periphery.

This familiarity with greatness, however, was shocked repeatedly over time, primarily as a result of the convulsive transitions between various Chinese governing dynasties. It took a particularly hard and grievous knock in the 19th century when a sclerotic domestic order combined with military weakness to produce one of the key drivers of modern Chinese nationalism, the "century of humiliation." Although the epoch of humiliation is conventionally dated as beginning with the unequal treaties signed with the British in 1842 after the First Opium War, China's relative decline as a great power in fact begins much earlier, when its leadership of the global economy started passing slowly to Europe, largely because of internal malaise and inertia. Unlike in Western Europe—where the evolution of the war-making absolutist state, the rise of new social classes such as the bourgeoisie, the institutional protection offered to private commercial activities, and the recrudescence of nationalism and reason all combined to produce a "take-off" that would make the European promontory the new center of the evolving global economic system—China's traditional elites, the bureaucracy and the landed gentry, were content to pursue what were their traditional rent-seeking activities focused on protecting inherited legal and customary privileges. These actions, although consistent throughout Chinese history, were made manifest in the early modern era through suffocating regulations, constraints on commercial activities, the creation of state monopolies, restrictions on international trade, and a persistent emphasis on the ancient classics to the neglect of the new modes of modern science. Each of these elements interacted viciously to produce on balance a stagnation relative to Europe between the 15th and the 18th centuries.

By the dawn of the 19th century, China's relative economic decline was not only conclusive but turning into an absolute decline that would pave the way for the national humiliations that followed. Thus, for example, between 1820 and 1952, a period that roughly coincides with the entire sequence of perceived indignities in modern Chinese history, the per capita product in China actually contracted even as the global economic product rose more than eight-fold to produce a three-fold increase in per capita income. China's share of the global product also fell from one-third to one-twentieth during this period, and its real per capita income fell from 90 percent to less than one-quarter of the world average. In contrast, U.S. per capita income grew nearly nine-fold, European income grew four-fold, and Japanese income grew more than three-fold during this same time. The internal disorder, rebellions, and civil war that dominated this period took a heavy toll on China's population and its level of welfare. This ataxia was further compounded by colonial intrusions that led to wars and defeats at the hands of Japan, Russia, and the European powers, which exacerbated these humiliations by exacting large financial indemnities.[3]

Not surprisingly, then, the older historical memories of the inextricable link between internal disorder and external vulnerability —memories rooted in the chaos of past dynastic transitions— were further reinforced in Chinese national consciousness. Even as this deep-rooted fear of domestic turmoil persists, however, there has always existed in China an equally insistent—and justified— conviction that China remains a natural great power because of its large size, huge population, and venerable history and that sustaining its prosperity and power would require, as it always has, a tranquil and pacified periphery. Despite the vicissitudes of the modern era, such a self-conception, which can be traced back at least to the time of Sun Yat-sen, appears to have endured over both the Nationalist and the Communist phases of the contemporary Chinese state. In fact, given Chinese history since the rise of colonialism, the reform era beginning with Deng Xiaoping can best be understood as a concerted effort to recover China's past greatness by comprehensively refurbishing the foundations of its national strength so that its next appearance on the global stage—this time as a modern great power rather than simply as a great and ancient civilization—would be both robust and enduring.

Given this goal, the contemporary reform effort in China has focused fundamentally on liberalizing the economic system through the creation of a relatively open market in order to generate the high rates of growth necessary for constructing the material foundations of national power. High levels of national output are a *sine qua non* for raising the quality of life of China's large population. These improvements in living standards, in turn, serve to increase savings, investment, and human capital formation, enhance productivity, and, most importantly, preserve domestic order through the Communist version of the social contract, whereby the population is induced to accept the Party's "rule by the few" so long as growing personal freedoms and economic prosperity become increasingly available to the many. High rates of economic growth are also essential for building the sinews of war necessary to defend China's territory and its larger political claims against a range of internal and foreign threats, while simultaneously giving notice of its arrival as a true great power.

The steady acquisition of material resources through undistracted economic growth over the past three decades has thus enabled the Chinese state to preserve relatively high levels of internal order and security and avert serious political challenges to the governing regime. And it has simultaneously strengthened the nation's military capacity to prevent internal secessionism and deter external threats—thereby protecting, from Beijing's vantage point, the environment necessary for continued economic growth. As a corollary to this objective, China's political leaders have generally sought to pursue a foreign policy that incarnates Deng's slogan of "peace and development" in multiple ways. These include: a deliberate effort to maintain amicable political relations with all of China's neighbors and especially with the major powers, without compromising on Beijing's core territorial and political claims; a purposeful restraint in the use of force in regard to the periphery and against more distant powers, even as China continues to pursue a comprehensive program of military modernization and remains ever ready to employ its combat capabilities to protect its strategic interests; and, finally, an intentional implementation of a non-ideological foreign policy designed to deepen ties with all countries that are critical for the success of China's economic transformation, either because they possess key resources or markets or because of their geostrategic significance.

The success of this strategy over the past thirty years, as witnessed by the unparalleled growth in China's power, influence, and importance, highlights several important facets that are worthy of notice.

To begin with, the evidence at the highest level of national direction suggests that—despite the common suspicion that Beijing's policies are often products of bureaucratic wrangling or intra-elite competition—China does have a coherent grand strategy centered on the accumulation of comprehensive national power. While there may be disagreements about when exactly such a grand strategy acquired formal significance, or how this grand strategy is reflected in specific regional or functional decisions, there is little doubt today that China has pursued a discernable grand strategy along at least two distinctive dimensions. First, its rulers have demonstrated a clear capacity for substantive rationality—that is, the ability to set sensible nationals goals pertaining to the pursuit of wealth and the acquisition of power in light of their appreciation of China's position in the international system as well as its external and internal constraints. Second, China's ruling elites have exhibited a remarkable capacity for instrumental rationality—that is, the ability to relate means to ends in regard to producing, controlling, and utilizing their national resources for the purpose of effectively promoting their vital interests against a wide variety of actual, potential, or presumed threats. Although the existence of a grand strategy in this sense does not by any means imply that Chinese leaders are mechanistically wedded to implementing some rigid and inflexible "master plan" for power maximization, their pursuit of comprehensive national power as a goal, combined with guided internal economic liberalization and the desire to maintain a pacific regional environment as the means, reflects a coherent grand strategy, which is ultimately little other than "a state's theory of how it can best 'cause' security for itself."[4]

Further, although the Chinese commitment to acquiring national power comprehensively relies on the presence of a stable security environment both at home and abroad, this does not translate either into a willingness to compromise on what are core Chinese interests or a neglect of the military capabilities required to protect these stakes should they be imperiled. In this connection, Beijing's core objectives must be judged to include protecting the regime against internal challengers, preventing successful secessionism by peripheral regions such as Tibet and Xinjiang, forestalling the formal independence of Taiwan, and defending China's homeland, borders, territorial claims, and extended interests against all regional and extra-regional threats. Although Deng and his successors have, therefore, abandoned Mao's emphasis on "war and revolution" in favor of "peace and development," they have not by any means rejected the necessity for acquiring the most potent military capabilities that money can buy. Rather, consistent with the hard realist streak that dominates Chinese strategic culture, Beijing has continued to emphasize the acquisition of advanced military capabilities and the technology necessary to produce these artifacts.

In other words, China has given notice that it will not become a "postmodern" great power, one that rejects the utility of organized violence in pursuit of self-regarding goals in favor of joint gains realized through cooperative means alone. What China has done instead is to "instrumentalize" martial prowess and subordinate it to the attainment of larger objectives. Learning from the Soviet experience about the perils of an over-militarized grand strategy, and from their own familiarity with the limits and failures of revolutionary Maoism, China's leaders have sought to limit their reliance on military instruments primarily to prevent fundamental political losses—although being ever ready to use armed force in such contingencies—while utilizing the respite gained from the consequent, and perhaps transitory, attenuation of security competition to achieve both their developmental and their military modernization goals unimpeded. From a power-transition perspective, China thus remains the perfect example of a weak but rising power that deemphasizes security competition presently because the unimpeded buildup of national power that results promises to place it in a far more opportune position when consequential military rivalries arise in the future.

Finally, the Chinese leadership recognizes that the accumulation of comprehensive national power involves lengthy periods of time—

decades, not years—and hence that the success of their grand strategy inevitably depends on their capacity to take the long view. Probably alone among the currently rising powers—or the existing great powers, for that matter—China has exhibited a remarkable capacity for strategic patience. Whether it be managing the existing discord with Taiwan, or the unsettled borders with major rivals like India and Japan, or coping with the most important strategic threat of all, the United States, China's diplomacy and strategy has consistently focused on shifting every subject of disagreement onto the back burner—so long as such actions do not seriously threaten either immediate or irretrievable losses. The calculus underlying such temporizing is that deferment not only deflects consequential threats and buys more time for Beijing to continue its growth in capabilities unhindered but, more importantly, puts off the moment of reckoning until the balance of power changes further in favor of China, thereby assuring it a better chance of securing those outcomes it desired in the first place.

The emphasis on not vitiating the political atmosphere in any way that might interrupt China's economic modernization only underscores the wisdom encapsulated in Deng's famous admonition, "do not seek leadership." This cautionary injunction, which finds reflection in different aphorisms such as "bide time" and "maintain a low profile," reflects the leadership's conviction that a China that advances incrementally and refuses to make waves will be best protected against the envy, fears, and depredations of other states while it traverses this "important period of strategic opportunity," in which it is still weak and potentially vulnerable, even while rising relative to others and to its own past. The present epoch, when China yet lies "between the times," thus provides an opportunity for Beijing to move prudently but purposefully to increase its "economic strength . . . national defense strength, and . . . national cohesiveness" in order to obtain "a more favorable position in the increasingly fierce competition in terms of overall national strength."[5]

The Kinder, Gentler Turn in Chinese Grand Strategy

While the success of China's grand strategy as described above remains a remarkable tribute to Deng Xiaoping's strategic vision, the unparalleled, and seemingly unstoppable, growth in China's power, influence, and importance during these past thirty years has brought with it an unintended consequence: increased regional and global anxieties about China's long-range goals and intentions. The fact that such fears continue to materialize throughout the Asian continent and in the United States, despite the Chinese leadership's best efforts to comply with Deng's exhortation to lie low, suggests that at least some realist verities about power politics continue to be convincing: that sharp increases in the material power of states, even when accompanied by profuse reassurances, have the capacity to unsettle other countries, especially if the rapidly growing entity is viewed as possessing an authoritarian regime, having incentives to engage in revanchist policies, or capable of disturbing the established distribution of power in consequential ways.

Because China remains a subject of concern on all three counts, significant apprehensions have surfaced throughout the Asia-Pacific region and in the United States that the continued growth of Chinese power could produce over the long term a formidable nation that threatens the physical security and political autonomy of other local states, locks up Asia's resources either through military stratagems or preclusive economic and political arrangements, impedes American access to and connectivity with the Asian continent, and in general ends up as a hegemon capable of dominating the Asian landmass and its internal and external lines of communication. Beijing's behavior toward the Southeast Asian states in the context of the disputes over the South China Sea and China's coercion of Taiwan, all during the 1990s when China's rise in power was just becoming evident, only accentuated these fears. If unmitigated, the strengthening of such perceptions could have led to the rise of new balancing coalitions against China. As Edward Luttwak lucidly explains the dynamic in another context, "when a powerful country becomes yet more powerful, its strength may drive the very weakest of its neighbors into a frightened neutrality or outright client status, but neighbors marginally more secure will instead be stimulated to build up their strength, and to cooperate with one another against the great antagonist that threatens them all."[6] Were such an outcome to materialize, it would end up exacerbating regional security competition and compelling Beijing into the one course of action that it has sought most desperately to avoid thus far: being diverted from economic growth into strategic rivalries at a time when its efforts at accumulating comprehensive national power are by no means complete.

Precisely to avoid such a derailment, Chinese grand strategy has taken a kinder, gentler turn in recent years. Clearly, the quest for comprehensive national power has not been abandoned. That objective remains the bedrock on which China's rise to greatness will have to be constructed. Without the expansive power deriving from economic growth, technological modernization, political stability, and growing military capacity, China would be unable to recover the geopolitical preeminence it has longed for and which remains the only instrument that would allow it to fully erase "the century of national humiliation" and take its place among the true great powers in the international system. The objective of the newest evolution in Deng's original grand strategy, therefore, aims at assuring China's continued growth in power-political capacity broadly understood while simultaneously preventing the emergence of balancing coalitions that might arise in response to such growth.[7]

Toward this end, China has developed a grand strategy that understandably persists with its traditional emphasis on economic transformation, but renews its approach to maintaining a peaceful external environment by explicitly integrating: a new doctrinal framework that affirms Beijing's "permanently" peaceful intentions; an emphasis on targeted good-neighbor policies designed to wean states, especially adjacent ones, away from potential balancing behaviors or coalitions; an effort to use China's growing economic strength as leverage to increase dependency on the part of potential rivals and neutrals throughout East, Southeast, South, Central, and Northern Asia; and a willingness to appease the reigning hegemon, the United States, at least until Beijing can more effectively cope with American power independently, while continuing to exploit any Asian dissatisfaction with Washington to enhance China's own counter-balancing goals. This refurbishing of Chinese grand strategy thus includes one significant departure from Deng's original approach. Recognizing that persisting with his strategy of lying low implies foregoing the opportunity to shape the strategic environment to Beijing's advantage, his contemporary heirs have embarked on a renewed effort to involve China on the global stage in order to simultaneously give notice of its incipient arrival as a great power; forge friendly relations with far flung states (for purposes of developing new allies and new access as well as to preempt various countries from aiding the United States against China down the line); secure stable supplies of critical natural resources necessary for its uninterrupted growth; and export Chinese culture as an instrument of legitimization and as a form of reassurance.

Given the rational nature of Chinese decision-making on grand strategic issues, it should not be surprising that Beijing has moved with some alacrity in each of these areas. For example, Chinese theoreticians associated with President Hu Jintao, most notably Zheng Bijian, have assiduously purveyed the doctrine of a "peaceful rise," which asserts that in contrast to the warlike behavior of ascending great powers of the past, the ascent of China as a modern great power will be entirely peaceful since the era of tight economic interdependence between China and its trading partners in Asia not only makes war unthinkable but actually allows all sides to "rise together" through peaceful trade and commerce. Although this formulation—based on classical liberalism and developed explicitly as an antidote to regional fears of a growing "China threat"—was repudiated as a result of power struggles between the Hu Jintao/Wen Jiabao and the Jiang Zemin/Zeng Qinghong factions of the Chinese Communist Party, the general idea still survives in transmuted formulations such as "peaceful development." Irrespective of which formulation is finally canonized, the fact that Beijing has gone to such lengths to produce this kind of theory clearly suggests that "China spends a lot of time worrying about what other countries think of it."[8]

China's new emphasis on good neighborly relations is also dramatically different from its behavior of the 1990s. Instead of stressing Chinese claims in territorial and maritime disputes as it did during that decade, Beijing today has made a special effort to assure its neighbors that China is a responsible and constructive partner. It has agreed to codes of conduct in those cases where territorial disputes have economic consequences (e.g., the South China Sea); it has begun negotiations, albeit at a glacial pace, to resolve border disputes that involve some important neighbors (e.g., India); it has started to take its nonproliferation obligations much more seriously than before (e.g., the White Paper on Nonproliferation); and it has expressed a willingness to shelve active political disputes that cannot be resolved immediately so long as none of the other parties involved disturbs the status quo (e.g., Taiwan).

In general, China has refocused its energies on expanding economic trade and cooperation with all its neighbors and, in a sharp departure from the past when China emphasized bilateral negotiations that accentuated its own strength, Beijing has now demonstrated a willingness to engage in multilateral diplomacy where its own power is ostensibly eclipsed (e.g., the Shanghai Cooperation Organization and the Asian Regional Forum). In some—important—instances, it has even taken the lead in complex multilateral issues of high politics (e.g., the "Six Party Talks" on North Korea), although such interventions continue to be dogged by anxieties about China's real objectives and their compatibility with those of its international partners. In general, the objective of China's recent good-neighbor policies, in line with the so-called New Security Concept unveiled in 1997, has been to develop friendly relations with all the major states on China's periphery—Russia, Japan, India, and the Central and Southeast Asian states—that are potential balancing partners in any future U.S.-led anti-Chinese coalition in Asia.

As part of its effort to defuse the growing perception of a Chinese threat, Beijing has gone out of its way to convince Washington that it has "neither the intention nor the capability" to challenge U.S. leadership in Asia, even as it seeks to promote a regional environment where an American political-military presence will eventually become unnecessary. Toward these ends, China has adopted a subtle multi-dimensional strategy vis-à-vis the United States and its allies. As far as the former is concerned, Beijing has used the global war on terror to position itself as an American partner, going out of its way to express solidarity with Washington even as it seeks to strengthen its economic, political, diplomatic, and military posture in Asia at American expense. As far as American allies like Japan, South Korea, Taiwan, Australia, and the minor Southeast Asian states go, China has used its gigantic economy to tighten the mutual embrace with these states such that each of them would be faced with the prospect of acute commercial losses were they to support any U.S.-led policies opposing China in the future. Equally relevant, China has exploited every sign of regional dissatisfaction with those overbearing American policies associated with the war on terror to cast itself as a friendly, non-interfering, and supportive alternative to U.S. power in the region. In this context, China has sought to promote new institutional arrangements in which it can exercise a leadership role, but that exclude the United States.

Finally, China has begun to look beyond the Asia-Pacific region knowing full well that if its growth in power is to proceed unhampered over time, it will have to make its presence felt beyond its immediate geographic confines. In the near term, this ranging afield has been driven primarily by the need to secure stable energy sources to fuel its dynamic economic machine. China, accordingly, has sent trade missions not only to Central Asia and the Persian Gulf, but to Africa and Latin America as well. As part of its growing international presence, however, China has become increasingly involved in issues of global governance, working through the United Nations and others to deal with matters ranging from drug trafficking to the environment to arms proliferation. China today participates in more than fifty international governmental organizations and more than a thousand international non-governmental organizations. More interestingly, China has become increasingly conscious of the need to promote its culture abroad both because of its public diplomacy advantages and because of its belief that a genuine appreciation of Confucian rectitude will go a long way toward mitigating suspicions about how Beijing might exercise its future power. Through such attempts at deepening its involvement in the global system, China has sought to reinforce the impression of being a constructive member of the global community. This effort is not only a response to the increasing American insistence that China become a "responsible stakeholder" in the international arena, but also contributes to assuaging the still-significant fears about China's long-term ambitions, while simultaneously helping to address some collective problems at minimal cost to Beijing.

Dealing with China as a Global Power: The Challenges Ahead

The evidence of the past three decades abundantly suggests that not only does China have a coherent grand strategy but also that it has adroitly adapted that strategy to meet the challenges of the times. When national interests required a singular self-regarding approach to advancing Chinese aims, Beijing's grand strategy produced the same. When mitigating foreign anxieties about China's growth in power became the issue, Beijing adjusted dexterously to alter its grand strategy accordingly. The current strategy of emphasizing peaceful ascendancy will therefore likely satisfy Chinese interests so long as it subsists "between the times," that is, while it still remains a weaker but rising power, not yet a true peer competitor of the United States. When that point is reached, however, a further evolution of China's grand strategy is inevitable. Whether that inflection takes the form of quiet or strident assertiveness, only time will tell—but there are few reasons to believe it could be otherwise.[9]

If it is possible to imagine that China's growth rates will remain positive for a long time to come, the prospect of a power transition within the international system becomes plausible. It is, of course, obvious that China will not be able to sustain the abnormally high growth rates witnessed during the past three decades indefinitely. The iron law of diminishing returns that neoclassical economics has explicated in exquisite detail ensures that Chinese growth rates will fall as its economy moves closer to full efficiency and reaches the technological frontier. But even if reduced, though still positive, growth rates are assumed to obtain—Angus Maddison, for example, assumes a 5.6 percent annual growth rate until 2010, a 4.6 percent annual growth rate between 2010 and 2020, and a little more than 3.6 percent annual growth from 2020 to 2030, for a total average annual growth rate of 4.5 percent between 2003 and 2030—the Chinese economy will at some point overtake the U.S. economy in size, when measured by purchasing power parity methods. On the basis of his assumptions, Maddison concludes that this will occur before 2015 and that the Chinese economy will constitute a full quarter of the global GDP by about 2030.[10]

To be sure, such assessments are always controversial: the size of the Chinese economy will continue to appear much smaller when measured by exchange rate methods (even though these are not ideal for international comparisons), and the basis for purchasing power parity measurements themselves could be revised periodically, thus resulting in adjustments of all inter-country comparisons. In any event, the protagonists of the overtaking thesis readily admit that even when the Chinese economy becomes the largest in the world, China's per capita income would still lag behind that of the United States—possibly remaining as low as one-third—not to mention Western Europe and Japan. Given all these complications, the prognosis of a genuine power transition occurring *in the prospective future* could itself become highly contestable. This, however, is an argument only about when a true transition would occur, not about whether it would occur at all. So long as the Chinese economy continues to grow at some rate faster than the American economy over a period of time, there will come a point where China begins to rival the United States by some universally acceptable standard of measuring power. It is during this phase—assuming that Beijing's current kinder, gentler approach is not disturbed in the interim—that Chinese grand strategy would likely further evolve in more assertive directions.

Such a turn toward assertiveness, understood at the very least as an insistent affirmation or an unswerving defense of its prerogatives, could arise because of factors peculiar to the Chinese experience: its historical memory of past greatness and the desire to restore previous eminence; its determination to erase the painful legacy of a century of national humiliation; its desire to recreate the traditional Sinocentric world order as a means of regulating the political and economic structures of super- and sub-ordination, at least in Pacific Asia if not beyond; and its belief that China's external security in the past was primarily assured by a strong state able to dominate, or at the very least neutralize, the strategic periphery. But the incentives for assertive behavior would also—and almost inevitably—arise as a result of the normal competition in world politics, the jostling that compels every state to continually seek increases in national power in an effort to preserve security. Since this competition takes place against both the backdrop of "the uneven growth of power among states"[11] and the actions that a rising state's regional and global competitors are certain to take in anticipation of its arrival as a serious challenger, it should not be surprising that ascending powers often adopt emphatic political postures as they struggle to restructure the existing international system to better support their own interests and claims. In other words, China's own relatively superior growth rates and the anxieties that such performance will induce in Japan, India, Russia, and the United States will compel most if not all these powers to adopt active balancing strategies that, as a consequence, will force China to respond by vigorously attempting to protect its emerging advantages in the face of what would be serious security competition.

At the very least, therefore, a powerful China that edges ever closer to the center of the global political system is unlikely to play the role of a "responsible stakeholder," as current U.S. policy has often demanded. Rather than dutifully upholding an international order that was designed primarily to protect American interests, a gradually powerful China would actually seek to weaken such an order—to the degree that it constrained Beijing's freedom of action—and replace it, probably in bits and pieces, with new political arrangements that had as their principal purpose the advancement of Chinese ambitions. These efforts, in turn, are liable to produce a Sino-American rivalry both in the Asia-Pacific region and at the core of the global system—an outcome that is most likely to ensue when China's acquisition of comprehensive national power is successful enough to make it a reasonable peer competitor of the United States. The assertiveness to be expected in these circumstances would in all probability become manifest only slowly and progressively—as a function of the gradual accretion in Chinese power—and not through some dramatic irruption that materializes soon after Beijing's national strength happens to cross a certain magical point on its growth trajectory.

In any event, it is difficult to offer precise predictions about how China would employ its expected assertiveness to restructure the international political system to its advantage, since that would depend not only on the general balance of power between Beijing and its competitors obtaining at the time, but also on the character of the regimes that govern all the relevant states, the nature of their interactions and the extent of their interdependence, and the quality of the critical civilian and military technologies of the era. These uncertainties notwithstanding, it is reasonable to postulate that as China becomes a true great power, odds are that it will behave like other great powers have in the past. If history offers any indications in this regard, it would not be surprising to see China augment its military capabilities in a manner that allows it to control, if not dominate, those regions, both near and far, that are deemed most critical to its security. Given the pressures of contemporary geopolitics, this would imply a concerted effort to establish mastery in the Asia-Pacific region and along Beijing's landward peripheries and then, depending on the available surplus of power, to maintain a modicum of influence, if not control, in more outlying areas that

42

connect this acknowledged Chinese "sphere of influence" with the wider world.

Within this zone of recognized preeminence, Beijing would seek to maintain relations with the regional states so as to ensure China's own vital interests as well as recognition by other states in the region of China's primacy. It would promote a steady diminution of Washington's role as a security provider—offering itself as the desirable substitute—and it would reject any vision of the United States as an "offshore balancer" because the residual presence and activities entailed by that conception would serve to limit the exercise of Chinese power along its peripheries. Sustaining this system of influence, however, will require China to engage in power politics on a global scale in order to prevent the United States and other competitors from consolidating their own power through similar arrangements elsewhere and thereby accumulating the necessary resources to resist China in Asia and abroad, even as it compels China to manage its own sphere of influence effectively enough to produce the material instruments and strategic coherence essential to successfully procure its desired outcomes worldwide.

Regional dominance and international success are, therefore, related "dialectically": they do not constitute competitive strategic goals, a consequential either/or, but rather are mutually reinforcing. China's evolution as the preponderant power in Asia—should its economic transformation be sustained over time—would thus be accompanied inevitably by the steady growth of its global impact through economic, diplomatic, and military instruments. Whatever its initial inclinations may have been, even if China is not forced along this path by its history and ambitions—and these arguably suffice in any case—it will almost inexorably be compelled to do so by the competitive structure of the international system, which will induce it to behave like any "ordinary" great power, even if it had originally sought to conduct itself as an "exceptional" one. The history of the United States is itself a fascinating testament to this "tyranny of the structure."

Under such circumstances, the political order in Asia would unavoidably, even if only gradually, become Sinocentric, and Sinic influence could extend to the entire globe over time, depending on what happens to the relative power of the United States and others in the interim. This dynamic does not rely on the assumption that China will consciously seek to construct a Sinocentric system on the basis of a "stealthy strategy towards global dominance."[12] Rather, that outcome will occur through a complex mixture of inadvertence, opportunism, externalities, and occasionally deliberate decision "simply" as a result of the uninterrupted accretion in Chinese national power relative to others. If China's emergence as a peer competitor finally materializes, it would in fact be shocking if Beijing, in contrast to every other great power capital in recorded history and its own behavior during past periods of preeminence, chose not to utilize its newfound power to advance its material interests, cement its status, and exercise its influence as a legitimate right. At the very least, therefore, China should be expected to ensure that every significant question in the realm of regional and global politics would be addressed, and hopefully resolved, only after its own interests have been taken into account.

As is to be anticipated, China's leaders today insistently deny any desire to behave "hegemonically." As the official spokesman of China's foreign ministry encapsulated their protestations, "China is a responsible country which takes the road of peaceful development. We will never pose any threat to any country or any people. Instead, we will strive for the peace and stability of the world so as to promote the development of ourselves, and vice versa. China will never seek hegemony, or threaten any other country."[13] Chinese Premier Wen Jiabao reiterated this theme even more emphatically when he declared that "China will never seek hegemony. Some people are worried that a stronger and more developed China would pose a threat to other countries . . . Such worry is completely misplaced . . . Even if we become stronger and more developed, we will not stand in the way of others, still less become a threat to others."[14] While Beijing's interest in maintaining this non-threatening profile in the current international order is eminently understandable—it is, after all, one precondition for the successful Chinese accumulation of national power—the reaffirmation that China will never "seek hegemony or world dominance" is less a function of Beijing's intentions now and more a function of how its own material capabilities grow vis-à-vis those of others over time—as the transformation of the United States from its own anti-imperial past to its manifestly imperial present would doubtlessly attest.

The persistence of international structural constraints—as the American example illustrates *a fortiori*—does not, however, imply the simplistic replication of strategic behaviors in every detail. The future international system, for example, is likely to be far more complex than the one that engendered the rise of American power. The presence of nuclear weapons, the realities of globalization, the crosscutting cleavages of ethnicity and ideology, the struggle between autocracy and democracy, and China's own domestic politics and culture will all intersect in complex fashion to simultaneously constrain and liberate China's political choices. None of these realities, however, will alter the one fundamental prediction that should be of relevance here: all great powers, China included, will constantly strive to increase their security, power, and influence by peaceful means whenever possible, and by contestation and the force of arms whenever necessary, so long as the international system remains "anarchic" in the sense understood since Thucydides. This reality, more than any other, is what will drive China to assert its power in Asia and beyond, even if it does not always do so in militant ways. Yet, the very prospect of such an occurrence is likely to make Sino-American relations competitive over the long term as both states come to represent a new bipolar ordering in international politics. Of course, bilateral relations could turn out to be conflict-ridden for many lesser reasons as well, and in considerable advance of the onset of bipolarity, but such competition would be attributed to the warp and woof of normal international politics and not to the challenges imposed by what John Gerard Ruggie once called its "deep structure."[15]

In any event, as China continues to successfully expand its national power over time, it is likely to be resisted by both its regional competitors and the United States, no matter how much it trumpets its doctrine of peaceful ascendancy. The evidence for such balancing, whether hard or soft, is already beginning to emerge. Major regional powers such as Japan and India, for example, are already initiating significant programs of military modernization as well as revitalizing their ties with Washington in expectation of an enhanced Chinese threat in the future. Even Russia, which historically has been Beijing's most important supplier of military equipment, now exhibits real consternation about what the diffusion of its advanced military technologies to China would imply for its own security. The Southeast Asian states, all much weaker than China and many lacking formal alliances with foreign powers, have embarked on a novel effort at enmeshing China in a multitude of regional institutions in order to induce moderation in Beijing's behavior and increase the costs of any future Chinese use of force—even as they engage Japan, India, and the United States as a form of insurance. Concerns about the rise of China, thus, appear to be increasingly manifest throughout Asia, and while this may appear to provide a propitious environment for containing Beijing as its accumulation of comprehensive power gathers steam, three inescapable challenges confront any such endeavor.

First, the vast growth of economic interdependence in Asia makes most of China's regional competitors diffident to challenge Beijing so long as the latter does not present a "clear and present danger" to them and so long as the presence of other non-military instruments continues to offer the hope of constraining China peacefully. While the military might of the United States today remains the best assurance that such diffidence will not translate into strategic vulnerability, it is not clear whether this will continue to be the case in a future bipolar system where Beijing increasingly becomes Washington's military peer across multiple indices of capability. This would be especially relevant if the United States, which would presumably stand to lose the most in relative terms as a result of growing Chinese power, found itself either weakened economically or ensnared in a tight economic embrace with China that produces strategic paralysis. The prospect of especially the latter—a deepening Sino-American trading relationship of the kind that was completely absent during the heyday of U.S.-Soviet rivalry—and China's emerging role as an important American creditor, not to mention the political power of key U.S. constituencies that profit from strong ties with China, will complicate any attempt by the United States to restrain the growth of Chinese capabilities in some straightforward fashion.

China's incipient centrality in the emerging Asian economic system, and the resulting gains from trade for the countries in its periphery, has also resulted in these states seeking to avoid making any stark choices between China and the United States—a preference that could persist even in the event of conflict between these two great powers. The net result of the emerging global economic order, in any case, is that rising, more-powerful states, such as China, can exploit the phenomenon of interdependence to increase their power and autonomy, even as their weaker partners become more reluctant to cut off their trading ties for fear of losing out in absolute terms. The tensions between the quest for power and the desire for plenty can thus make successful balancing more difficult—just when it may be most needed.

Second, the success of China's search for comprehensive national power threatens to progressively undermine the traditional American security system in Asia by producing shifts in all the relevant balances of power. The historic U.S. approach to providing security in Asia hinged on a "hub and spoke" system of bilateral security alliances. Its success derived from the presence of a certain local balance of military capabilities between the regional states married to Washington's unchallenged ability to protect its clients when necessary without any threat to the credibility of its commitments. The growth of Chinese military power since the 1990s—precipitated initially by a desire to protect its interests in Taiwan but now driven by the necessity of fielding a competent military commensurate with its rising status—will increasingly put at risk both elements of the security system that traditionally ensured stability in Asia. The induction of a significant force of short-range and medium-range ballistic missiles (many of consequential accuracy); the integration of what will soon be the largest contingent of fourth-generation combat aircraft in Asia supported by new airborne early warning and air refueling systems; the development of new offensive capabilities in the form of new cruise missilery, electronic warfare and computer network attack capabilities, and counter-space technologies; the selective modernization of certain land and naval forces relevant to frontier operations and power projection along the periphery; the construction of a national command, control, communications, and intelligence (C^3I) system involving multiple and redundant technologies; and the impressive modernization of military infrastructure, improvements in defense industrial capacity, changes in military organization, and adoption of new doctrines for combat operations, all presage a shift in the local balance of power against China's regional rivals. Although these states will respond to China's increasing capabilities with counter-acquisitions of their own, Beijing would be in a much stronger position to apply military force successfully against major competitors such as Japan and India (not to mention the minor powers of Southeast Asia) as its own combat capabilities mature over the next few decades. The superior growth that is presumed to characterize China's economic performance relative to its Asian rivals would only bestow on it further advantages in this regard.

Even as the local balance of capabilities changes to the disadvantage of the other Asian states, Beijing has already made tremendous strides toward undermining the other component of the traditional U.S. security system in Asia: holding at risk America's forward-deployed and operating forces and raising the costs of implementing U.S. security guarantees to its partners in the region. It is in this arena that the most significant changes have taken place, and these are certain only to accelerate as China continues its march toward becoming a true great power comparable to the United States. Whereas just twenty years ago Washington could deploy, reinforce, and operate its military forces along the Asian rimlands with impunity, and could conduct classic power-projection operations against the Chinese mainland without significant opposition, Beijing's evolving sea and aerospace denial, counter-intelligence, surveillance, reconnaissance, and nuclear modernization programs ensure that such achievements will no longer be easy. To be sure, the United States would still come out victorious in the event of any unlimited conflicts with Beijing today, but whether this outcome would obtain in an age of Chinese parity is quite doubtful. Equally important, in the more relevant and the more likely possibility of a limited war today—where all manner of political and temporal constraints would operate—an American victory, though still probable, would come at significantly higher costs. That this result would be even harder to obtain in an age of bipolarity seems close to obvious. The evolving deterioration in the strategic balance to America's disadvantage—and deterioration is exactly what it is—will therefore only be exacerbated as China's comprehensive national power increases over time. When China approaches peer status to become a true great power, it must be anticipated that this deterioration, which would find reflection in Beijing's ability to control the battle space in all dimensions at some distance from its frontiers while applying offensive power successfully against near and distant threats, will affect the credibility of U.S. security guarantees and, by implication, Washington's capacity to effortlessly orchestrate an Asian balancing coalition when required.

Third, and finally, a China that becomes a great power will behave as one—as a true pole in the international system—and, hence, will employ all the instruments that great powers have used throughout history to defeat prospective balancing coalitions whenever they threatened to materialize. Given Beijing's still-significant material weakness today, it is difficult to imagine how exactly this game would unfold because current Chinese inter-state behavior is still characterized largely by reactive decisions associated with its rising, but still vulnerable, profile. Recognizing what China would do when it became a genuine great power at the core of the global system, therefore, requires a leap of imagination that is often difficult because the details required to vivify its actions are not yet available. This fact notwithstanding, there is enough historical evidence to suggest that rising powers in the past have often adroitly exploited the burdens of balancing to defeat this dynamic in multiple ways: first, by masking the increases in their power capability; second, by making "side payments" to some pivotal states to neutralize emerging efforts at external balancing; and third, by pursuing temporarily accommodative policies, either selectively or overall, to preempt coalition formation until certain thresholds of power accumulation are decisively crossed.

Contemporary Chinese discussions about power politics suggest that elites in Beijing are aware of all these stratagems, and the record of the last ten years or so suggests that China's leaders are in fact capable of utilizing these approaches quite skillfully. As China grows in national strength, the necessity of using such alliance-breaking strategies would diminish in theory because Beijing's greater accumulated power would provide it with more direct coercive options, should it choose to utilize them. The benefits of exploiting such alternatives transparently, however, would always warrant careful and continuous review, particularly because their use, or overuse, could in fact tip the scales to generate the very opposing coalition that Beijing sought to preempt. Mindful of the fact that a rival United States—whether it is declining or holding on to its relative power—would be ever-interested in orchestrating balancing coalitions should the growth of Chinese power increase absolutely over time, it is likely that China would choose to use its by-now even more substantial resources to engage in alliance-breaking efforts whenever it concludes that its military instruments are either too expensive or incapable of procuring the political goals it seeks. The important point of note is this: the United States simply cannot afford to be complacent in assuming that a balancing coalition against Chinese power will readily form merely because Beijing manages to accumulate threatening levels of national power relative to its neighbors and the international system. Balancing is invariably a costly exercise and its fruits are never enjoyed symmetrically by all its beneficiaries. Hence, there is a constant temptation to "free ride" and, as a result, under-produce the very goods that may be critical to common security. This reality accounts for the repeated episodes of successful empire formation in history—an insight that, though often misunderstood by neorealists, ought not to elude policymakers in Washington.

On balance, therefore, these three realities suggest that coping with China as a global rival will be a challenging endeavor for the United States. Thanks to its great size, China will be a far more formidable competitor than Germany was in the early half of the 20th century. And thanks to China's deep connectivity with the international economic system, including the United States, the obvious containment strategies that worked so effectively vis-à-vis the Soviet Union in the latter half of the 20th century are unlikely to lend themselves to successful replication. Dealing with an emerging China will, therefore, require strategies quite unlike those that are familiar from the past. Above all else, Washington will need patience, subtlety, strategic flexibility, and the ability to hold the competing instruments of engagement, hedging, and balancing in a "reflexive equilibrium" that is capable of adapting rapidly, while at the same time rebuilding the domestic capacities required to sustain America's current preeminence and actually increase its margins of advantage to the extent possible. This effort will of necessity be long and involved. But given that China's leaders appear determined to stay in the competition and pursue the rational policies required for success, the United States, both for its own sake and for the sake of others who depend on it for their security, should do no less.

CHAPTER THREE

DETERRING CHINA

Old Lessons, New Problems

Dan Blumenthal

Amerrican strategists and Sinologists are relatively sanguine about America's capacity to deter China from employing military force against either its neighbors or the United States. This confidence is derived largely from two sources: the Cold War success of America's strategic competition with the Soviet Union and realist theories about the existing balance of power between the United States and China.

At first glance, there are certainly good reasons for this confidence. In the first instance, two ideologically inimical, nuclear-armed superpowers stood nose to nose for some four decades yet never directly raised a hand against each other. Realists, meanwhile, point to the fact that although China is a rapidly rising power, it still plays second fiddle to the U.S. in overall economic and military strength. China's leaders, it is argued, would have to be foolish to start a conflict that they are likely to lose. As one leading scholar has argued, "deterrence is stable in the Strait" today, because: (1) the Chinese understand their military inferiority; (2) the United States maintains escalation dominance at all levels of warfare; (3) China prefers to maintain the status quo; and (4) China believes in U.S. resolve to fight a war if necessary. As a result, Washington and Beijing have entered into an "easily established [relationship] of mutual deterrence that [provides] not only a buffer against general war, but also a strong constraint on both limited war and crisis behavior."[1]

But the foregoing analysis rests on two broad assumptions. First, that the lessons of the Cold War are, in fact, clear, and second, that the realist's account of state behavior fully captures China's own strategic calculus.

The "Lessons" of the Cold War

Since successful deterrence is defined by what does not happen, the lessons to be learned from the Cold War experience may be less than meet the eye. As Henry Kissinger writes:

> The Nuclear Age turned strategy into deterrence, and deterrence into an intellectual exercise. Since deterrence can only be detected negatively, by events that do *not* take place, and since it is never possible to demonstrate why something has not occurred, it became especially difficult to assess whether the existing policy was the best policy or just a barely effective one.[2]

Although it is a fact that the Soviets did not attack the United States or Western Europe, there may be many reasons—some obvious, others less so—for why that did not happen.

A closer look at the lessons of the Cold War suggests we should be somewhat cautious when attempting to apply them to the current U.S.-China relationship. First, to the extent that there was strategic stability during the Cold War, it was not a product of Moscow and Washington simply accepting the doctrine of mutual assured destruction (MAD), and freezing weapons development and strategic planning. Both sides engaged in a constant effort to improve their strategic arsenals, operations, and planning, never fully confident that their opponent was not gaining some critical advantage. Notably, this was the case both before and after arms-control agreements were signed. The result was a decades-long arms race.

Moreover, it was not clear that the Soviet Union ever fully signed on to what we in the West took to be the clear and compelling logic of MAD.[3] The assumption was that Soviet leaders would make the same cost-benefit calculations as we in the West would: they would not risk the use of nuclear weapons if they risked losing their own country in return. But scholars debated, and continue to debate, whether in fact the Soviets thought about nuclear war in this way and whether they believed that such a war could be fought—and won.[4]

Second, the United States discovered that nuclear primacy does not provide a clear coercive capability. As John Lewis Gaddis writes about the Cuban missile crisis: "Despite overwhelming nuclear supremacy—the United States had between eight and seventeen times the number of usable nuclear weapons that the Soviet Union did—the prospect of even one or two Soviet missiles hitting American targets was sufficient to persuade Kennedy to pledge . . . that he would make no further attempts to invade [Cuba]."[5] Nor, as Washington discovered, does nuclear primacy deter a competitor from pursuing its objectives through lesser forms of violence. As Kennedy and his successors learned, having the upper hand when it came to strategic nuclear capabilities did not prevent Moscow from supporting armed conflicts against Western interests in Southeast and Central Asia, Africa, and Central America.

Third, upon reflection, we now know that the role of individual leaders was of utmost importance in avoiding war. Khrushchev eventually walked away from the nuclear brink and Gorbachev real-ized that the Soviet Union could not survive while it was locked into a strategic competition with the Americans. It is impossible to know whether other Soviet leaders, such as Stalin or Andropov, would have reached similar conclusions.

Finally, during the Cold War, deterrence was only one, albeit im-portant, element in an overall policy of containment. Except perhaps during a period in the 1970s when détente ruled supreme, American policymakers believed that the competition with the Soviet Union would be ongoing and protracted. It was thought that Moscow would take almost any opportunity to challenge and, if possible, weaken the United States. Accordingly, America's deterrence posture was not thought of in isolation from other policies but was an integral ele-ment of its overall goal of containing the Soviet Union. The general policy framework within which deterrence was conducted made a difference. There was little doubt in the Kremlin's eyes that we saw the Soviets as a rival and, in that context, American threats had a high degree of credibility.

One should be cautious, then, in attempting to overlay the prin-ciples of deterrence as applied during the Cold War to the situation the U.S. faces with China today. In spite of our tendency to look back on the Cold War era as one of strategic stability, the reality was quite different. Deterrence was never easy to maintain and its ability to prevent conflict was more limited than many thought. Moreover, whatever the benefits of deterrence during the Cold War, they were contingent on particular leaders making decisions at critical times and, more broadly, were grounded in a policy of containment that kept deterrence uniquely at the front and center of the development of U.S. policy.

Getting Real about Realism

It is certainly true that a state that is stronger militarily and economi-cally is more likely to deter a weaker power than not. But there are also plenty of examples (both ancient and modern) of weak states initiating conflicts with stronger states. For example, Pyrrhus's campaign against Rome in 275 BC; Prussia's campaign against Austria in the Seven Years' War; Japan's attack on Russia in 1904; the Japanese attack on Pearl Harbor in 1941; the Pakistani offensive against India in 1965; Egypt's Sinai offensive in 1973; the Argentine invasion of the Falklands in 1982; and so on.[6] And, indeed, there are examples of the weaker defeating the stronger throughout history as well.[7]

The reality is that sometimes a weaker state can convince itself that its military is a better fighting force, its generals more savvy, or that an adversary simply has no stomach for a fight. It can also believe that by striking quickly and decisively, it can present a fait accompli to the world and its opponent before that opponent can marshal his greater resources. Sometimes the weaker power is simply dissatisfied with the status quo and believes that by bringing on a conflict it will reshuffle the international diplomatic deck of cards. And finally, for reasons of regime legitimacy, a state's leadership may well decide that risking defeat on the battlefield is worth the price. In short, being the superior power does not guarantee immunity from a military challenge.

To maintain deterrence, then, it is absolutely critical that one be as clear-headed as possible about a potential adversary, even if that adversary is the weaker power. In the end, deterrence is concerned primarily with influencing foreign minds and creating a set of conditions by which the opponent's leadership decides to be deterred. As Colin Gray notes, deterrence has as its goal "persuading an adversary not to take action that it might otherwise have done. Whether or not the intended object of the deterrence decides he is deterred is a decision that remains strictly in his hands."[8] Hence, understanding a potential attacker's perceptions, values, and political priorities is essential to a successful deterrence strategy.[9]

Moreover, as Fred Iklé has observed, when it comes to nuclear deterrence:

In the real world, nuclear forces are built and managed not by two indistinguishable 'sides,' but by very distinct governments and organizations. These in turn are run by people, people who are ignorant of many facts, people who can be gripped by anger or fear, people who make mistakes—sometimes dreadful mistakes.[10]

Finally, in trying to deter a potential adversary, a government must take into account that country's military and strategic history.[11] How and why has that country used force in the past? What are the continuities and discontinuities with that country's strategic tradition? Answering these questions can help to avoid the dangerous pitfall of applying a one-size-fits-all deterrence theory.

Given the complex array of factors that contribute to deterrence, it should come as no surprise that the stronger state has not always prevented a less powerful state from going to war with it. Before Pearl Harbor, for example, when tensions with Japan were clearly rising, it still was the consensus view in Washington that an all-out war was, in Henry Stimson's words, "the very last thing which the Japanese government desires" and, hence, the U.S. was free to try to squeeze Japan into negotiations by applying new economic sanctions.[12] And while Tokyo also understood that it could not tolerate those sanctions for long, Washington failed to properly assess both Japan's aversion to sacrificing its larger ambitions in Asia and the Japanese military's belief that it could fight a limited war with the United States. Japan's goal was not to engage the U.S. in a long and protracted fight, but to prevent it from interfering in the Japanese consolidation of its Asian conquests by striking a crushing first blow at Pearl Harbor and in the Philippines—in essence, handing Washington a fait accompli.[13]

Nor did Israel anticipate that Anwar Sadat was ready to launch a limited war for limited objectives in 1973. According to Kissinger, "what literally no one understood was the mind of the man: Sadat aimed not for territorial gain but for a crisis that would alter attitudes into which the parties were then frozen—and thereby open the way for negotiation."[14] Israel assumed that Egypt would look at the state of the military balance between the two countries and acknowledge the futility of engaging a superior adversary. Instead, although the Egyptians "did not anticipate a decisive victory, the expectation was that whatever tactical gains Egypt would make in the limited war could be used for a politically favorable settlement in the future."[15] A nuclear-armed Israel failed to deter Sadat because it did not entertain the possibility that considerations apart from a conventional view of the military balance would enter into his calculations.

Similarly, the fact that Britain had a military capability far superior to the Argentines did not prevent the latter from trying to take the Falklands in 1982. Having been in negotiations with the Argentine government about the status of the Falklands for years, London had proposed few concrete ideas for resolving the issue and, indeed, at various times had sent different signals about its determination to defend its possession. As T.V. Paul has noted, "The British expected no major military challenge and therefore did not make an immediate deterrent threat or show a willingness to resolve the underlying dispute with concessions that would have been sufficient to reassure Argentina. . . . [The result] was rather 'strategic ambivalence.'" This, in turn, led to the Argentine government doubting that the British were willing to pay the price for defending these out-of-the-way, seemingly strategically insignificant islands. A quick invasion and London would be forced to negotiate—or so the junta believed.[16]

The question is, does Washington risk repeating similar misjudgments when it comes to China?

A Different Strategic Framework

As noted above, Washington's overall objective vis à vis China differs markedly from the policy goal it had for the Soviet Union during the Cold War. While deterrence of the Soviet Union occurred in the framework of a policy of containment, for most of the past two decades Washington has adopted a policy of engagement with China. By incorporating Beijing into political, economic, and security relationships, the United States and other established powers hope China will learn and accept the basic norms of the prevailing international system, believing that any revisionist impulses China has will be overcome by enmeshing it in a system from which it gains concrete benefits.

At the same time, albeit more quietly, Washington has been following a hedging policy with China, the characteristics of which include an increased deployment of naval and air assets in the Pacific, an upgrading of alliances and relationships with states neighboring China (namely, Japan, Singapore, Vietnam, and India), statements "opposing" China's use of force in the Taiwan Strait, and prohibitions on sales of military items to the PRC.[17]

The "engage but hedge" policy is guided by an optimism that, on the one hand, the enmeshment of China in the international system will provide Beijing with incentives for peace, and, on the other, that the might of the American military can dissuade China from choosing a more aggressive course. Arguably, each prong of the policy has seen some success. China is now a major player in the global economy, and has joined an impressive array of regional and international institutions that would seem to give it a stake in the current world order. On the deterrence side of the equation, China has not attacked Taiwan.[18]

The core of the deterrence argument is that China has neither the desire nor the means to change the status quo by using force against Taiwan. Beijing has no desire to attack the island, the argument goes, because it is beset by internal problems and it needs, above all, a peaceful environment for continued economic growth. And it doesn't want to get into a conflict with the United States for the simple reason that the U.S. remains superior in conventional and strategic military capabilities.

This argument, of course, rests on the assumption that China's strategic calculations are very much along the lines of our own. But is that the case? Are there elements in China's own strategic tradition that should make us less confident when it comes to predicting when and how China might employ force?

The Chinese Strategic Tradition

Recent work on the history of Chinese strategic thinking has called into question the conventional wisdom that China's Confucian-Mencian tradition made for a peaceful strategic culture.[19] Analysis of the historical record has demonstrated that Chinese regimes have almost always had a martial component. By one count, China engaged in 3,790 internal and external wars from 1100 BC to the end of the Qing Dynasty in 1911. During the Ming Dynasty (1388–1644) alone, China engaged in an average of 1.12 external wars each year.[20] The majority of these wars were fought early in each regime's existence, and typically against countries and entities along China's periphery, a pattern the Chinese Communist Party (CCP) regime has maintained.[21] These campaigns typically aim to eliminate existing or potential threats to trade routes or frontiers, regain territory lost to foreigners, reinforce the regime's authority over "vassal" states, or reaffirm the regime's authority among its own people.

While the Chinese typically enjoyed military superiority relative to their adversaries, there are instances in which Chinese regimes confronted opponents they knew to be more powerful. For example, in the midst of the Cultural Revolution and in the face of overwhelming Soviet conventional and nuclear superiority, Mao instigated a series of military provocations that led to significant armed clashes at Zhenbao Island. (At the time, there were almost one and a half million Chinese and Soviet troops deployed along the border, and both sides were apparently prepared for possible nuclear confrontation.) Mao worried that Moscow intended to apply the Brezhnev Doctrine to China, and deemed the prospect of a military defeat to be more palatable than subservience to the Soviets.[22]

Similarly, in 1979, Deng Xiaoping started a war with Vietnam without being sure that his forces would hold the upper hand—and for reasons that would not traditionally be recognized as justifying war. First, Deng was interested in using the conflict as a way of consolidating his leadership position over Hua Guofeng, Mao's successor and Deng's predecessor. Second, Deng wanted to teach Vietnam, a former tributary state, a lesson after its invasion of Cambodia, a Chinese ally. In doing so, he also wanted to show Hanoi that Moscow, Vietnam's principal backer, was not a reliable ally. And finally, after repeated Vietnamese incursions into disputed border areas, he wanted to demonstrate to the world that China was serious about territorial issues.[23] China launched the war despite the presence of substantial Soviet forces on its northern border and in the face of a Vietnamese army that was battle-tested and intent on defending its own territory. Ultimately, Deng gambled successfully that his actions would be just forceful enough to attain some of his political objectives but not provocative enough to trigger a Soviet response.[24]

Just as threats of superior force have not deterred Chinese leaders, neither has domestic turmoil prevented the People's Republic from going to war. When China's leaders made the decision to use force against the United States and its allies in Korea in 1950, against the Soviets in 1969, and against Vietnam in 1979, the Chinese state was not only internally weak but was either in the midst of a crisis or just emerging from one. In each case, China's leaders used force not only to secure traditional state interests, but also to consolidate their position and mobilize the population.[25]

The above examples demonstrate that the PRC has not always waited to achieve military superiority or even parity before attacking its adversaries; nor has China shied away from using force for purposes that we in the West would not ordinarily consider legitimate. This history should make American policymakers a little less sanguine in their capacity to predict the conditions under which China will use force in the future.

How the Current Leadership Thinks About Strategy and Force

What do China's leaders make of their country's martial history? Is it a tradition they share? Is the current generation of Chinese leaders substantially different from those that preceded them?

The short answer is that we simply don't know. American intelligence officials, policymakers, and strategists lack an understanding of, to use Alexander George's terminology, the "operational code"—that is, a government's beliefs about "the nature of politics and political conflict, [their] views regarding the extent to which historical developments can be shaped . . . [and] notions of correct strategy and tactics"—of today's Chinese leadership.[26] While the Cold War generated a voluminous body of scholarship on the Kremlin's strategic vision, its notions of statecraft, its bureaucratic ethos, and its perceptions of the West, there is no equivalent body of knowledge available to American policymakers dealing with China.

Of course, that lack of information has not prevented analysts from arguing that the current leadership is a breed apart from its predecessors. Specifically, this set of leaders is said to be technocratic and pragmatic. China is no longer led by passionate revolutionaries who can single-handedly shape strategic thinking regarding the use of force.[27] Today, there are said to be more divisions within the CCP leadership over the utility of force—reportedly, the leadership debated and then rejected using some form of military coercion against Taiwan in 1999 and 2004.[28]

The common portrayal of China's president and party head, Hu Jintao, is that he is a leader averse to risk-taking who must still fight to maintain control of the Party. In addition, Hu and Premier Wen Jiabao are said, because of their experiences in the Cultural Revolution, to be more attuned to the social and economic inequalities now plaguing China than to issues of national greatness.[29] Hu and Wen's priority is to create a "harmonious society" by leveling the social playing field and remedying the excesses brought about by China's adoption of a capitalist economic system.

But for all the pragmatism supposedly at the heart of the so-called "third" and "fourth generation" of Chinese leadership, it is striking that neither President Hu nor his predecessor, Jiang Zemin, slowed the pace of the PLA's modernization—or, for that matter, shied away from demonstrations of force.

Indeed, it was under Jiang that China engaged in coercive diplomacy to influence Taiwan's presidential elections. Jiang also engaged in military muscle-flexing in disputed territories in the South

China Sea; China and Vietnam had naval contretemps in 1992 and 1994; the Chinese navy seized Mischief Reef from the Philippines in February 1995; and Chinese demonstrations of force in the South China Sea continued into the late 1990s.[30]

Hu has also proved he is capable of being tough. He established his Party credentials by clamping down on Tibet when he was Party secretary in the late 1980s, and since becoming president he has not hesitated to put down protests and increase controls over the press, use of the Internet, and NGO activities. He has warned that "the Soviet Union disintegrated under the assault of their Westernization and bourgeoisie liberalism" and also warned against the dangers lurking from outside sources as exhibited by the "color revolutions" of Georgia and Ukraine.[31]

It would also be inaccurate to characterize Hu's management of military affairs as entirely risk-averse. Under his watch, the PRC has deployed naval power to disputed areas of the East China Sea, used its submarines to probe the waters in and around Japan, and even deployed a Chinese sub to harass an American carrier.[32] In January 2005, Japan spotted two Chinese navy missile destroyers in the waters near the Japan-China median line, cruising toward an ocean survey vessel chartered by Japan.[33] In September 2005, Japanese intelligence detected a flotilla of Chinese warships near a Chinese gas rig "exploiting resources in the East China Sea that are claimed by Japan."[34] The East China Sea has also hosted two of China's largest joint military exercises, including joint naval and air force exercises with Russia in August 2005. And finally, under Hu, the PRC passed the "Anti-Secession Law" that permits "non-peaceful" means to resolve the Taiwan issue, while continuing to develop and deploy an impressive array of military power opposite Taiwan.

China is "also acutely sensitive to domestic and external challenges to its stability and status."[35] Indeed, the country is beset by internal unrest, a situation it fears that outside powers will take advantage of. As one scholar has written, "in past crises, Chinese leaders have been prepared to go to significant lengths to avoid the appearance of being weak and giving in to great-power pressures or of engaging in overtly predatory or manipulative behavior themselves."[36]

In short, the view that China has turned a corner when it comes to how it thinks about the use of military force is based less on what we really know and more on what we hope to be the case. There are, of course, good reasons for China not to find itself involved in a conflict. Nevertheless, from what we know of China's history and what little we know of today's leadership, there is no reason to believe that China's strategic operational code has fundamentally changed—and some reason to believe that it remains largely the same.

The Taiwan Issue

From the U.S. perspective, it seems rational that the Chinese would eschew conflict over Taiwan in order to advance other, seemingly more important, national goals. But do the Chinese share that perspective?

To start, there are strong nationalist pressures on the CCP to reverse the "century of humiliation" and "reunify the motherland." The return of Hong Kong and Macau to Chinese control in 1997 and 1999 were important landmarks in China's recent history. But in the minds of the Chinese, of course, this makes the fact that Taiwan remains independent of the mainland even more galling. Taiwan has now become a critical litmus test of the regime's nationalist credentials—and hence, the leadership's very legitimacy.[37] It is unclear how long the CCP can or even wants to hold back those pressures. If it is true that the regime's survival is the paramount goal of the CCP, and that the loss of Taiwan would threaten the regime, it is difficult to imagine that China could indefinitely tolerate Taiwan's de facto independence.

Moreover, China has for centuries viewed Taiwan as a potential security threat. Qing rulers viewed the island with concern as it sometimes served as a staging area for attacks on the mainland and Chinese trade. In reaction, China's rulers encouraged Han migration to Taiwan in order to consolidate control over the island. And precisely because of its strategic location—just off China's coast and just south of Japan—Taiwan, in turn, became a focal point for Sino-Japanese rivalry.[38] As early as 1871, Japan launched an attack on Taiwan and eventually forced China to cede the island after defeating the mainland in the Sino-Japanese War in 1895.[39]

With the Communist victory over the Chinese Nationalists (Kuomintang) in 1949 and the Nationalists' ensuing retreat to Taiwan, the "reunification of the motherland" became an important CCP objective. For Mao, it would mark the definitive victory, ending the Chinese civil war. The fragile new party-state, fearful of both internal and external attempts to rob it of its success, saw Taiwan as the seat of both. As Taiwan became the home to the Kuomintang government and an outpost of American influence in the East, the Chinese leadership saw the island as both a contagion of imperialist capitalism and as a threat to the young Communist regime's survival. Mindful that the loss of Taiwan to Japan became one of the most powerful symbols of the Qing Dynasty's impotence, Mao further feared that his failure to reclaim the island would be seen in a similar light.

President Harry Truman's 1950 declaration that "the occupation of Formosa by Communist forces would be a *direct threat* to the security of the Pacific Area"[40] and to United States forces increased Mao's fears of an impending American attack on the mainland. As the Seventh Fleet sailed into the strait, it became clear that the United States had equated Taiwan's security with its own. Unable to confront the overwhelming U.S. military advantage, Mao and Zhou En-lai responded by calling off any attack on Taiwan and preparing defensive positions along the coast.[41]

By the 1990s, Taiwan no longer represented a military threat to the mainland—its leaders had eschewed all claims of being the sole legitimate government of China and, reflecting that fact, Taiwan had begun cutting its military budget. Now Taiwan's threat to China was of a different character. First, Beijing worried that Taiwan's separation from the mainland and decreasing interest in uniting with the mainland would instigate "Taiwan separatism" in other parts of the Chinese empire, such as Tibet or Xinjiang. Second, in supporting Taiwan, Beijing believed that the United States and Japan were intentionally frustrating China's own rise and the completion of the reintegration of China's "lost" territories.

In a sense, the Chinese were right about Taiwan. It is now a democracy, and only a small percentage of its citizens identify themselves as being simply Chinese. They overwhelmingly believe themselves to be a sovereign, independent nation. In Beijing's mind, the real task is to stop the gradual process of Taiwan consolidating its de facto independence. To halt this trend and, indeed, reverse it, the PRC has employed two policies: increasing economic ties with the island and military intimidation. But there is little evidence that economic integration is, in fact, leading to political integration, as the Chinese had hoped. Taiwanese companies certainly want to do business in China and, as such, desire stable relations, but few, if any, business leaders see unification as a desirable end. As a result, one has to ask whether the prospect for Chinese military action against Taiwan will grow as the PRC leadership recognizes that its policies are not leading to real change on the island.

And, indeed, the PLA has been tasked with developing military options to deal with that eventuality. Since 1996, the PRC has been conducting more and more realistic annual military exercises at Dongshan, across from Taiwan, to run through what would be required in an invasion scenario. PRC spokesmen and PLA generals repeatedly remind Taiwan that "the PLA is capable and confident of settling the Taiwan issue by force."[42]

These exercises, together with China's rapid military modernization, have caused Washington, Taipei, and the rest of the region to take Chinese threats about Taiwan seriously and have led to a number of new initiatives in U.S. policy. First, the U.S. has sought to avoid situations in which a military confrontation might arise and, in turn, to pursue its policy of engagement with China even more assiduously.[43] Second, the U.S. has begun to work more closely with Taiwan's military in order to improve its defensive capabilities.

Third, Washington has been more assertive in restraining Taiwan and chastising it for any statements or policies that might be taken as a move toward asserting its independence.[44]

It is unclear just how far these initiatives have advanced Washington's deterrence objectives in the region. On the one hand, ever since Washington sent carriers to the strait in 1996, Beijing has concluded that it must plan for—and hopefully deter—a U.S. intervention on behalf of Taiwan should a conflict occur. On the other hand, by suggesting that there are situations in which the United States would not come to Taiwan's defense—vaguely defined as Taiwan violating the "status quo"—Washington indirectly fuels Beijing's sense of entitlement with respect to Taiwan and cracks the door open for Chinese military action.

Moreover, the U.S. has above all else sought to ensure that any resolution of Taiwan's status occurs peacefully, but remains formally agnostic as to the outcome. It must seem odd (and perhaps not credible) to Beijing that Washington would fight a war with China in order to protect the principle of "non-use of force" in a dispute in which it has repeatedly claimed indifference toward the final substantive resolution.

America's Deterrence Options

For U.S. policymakers, the requirements of deterring China are multifaceted and challenging. First, the U.S. has not adopted a Cold War-style policy of containment for China. As a result, America's deterrence capabilities and signaling must be managed within a more complex set of relations.

Second, the United States is committed to a peaceful resolution of the Taiwan issue. Yet there is no resolution in sight. The U.S. insists on maintaining what it calls the "status quo" even while the average Taiwanese grows less and less interested in uniting with the mainland and the average Chinese grows ever more insistent that the island be returned to the motherland. Toss in the fact that the "status quo" itself is left undefined and the possibility of misunderstanding and miscalculation is significant. There is, in other words, no Fulda Gap when it comes to what might spark a conflict in the Taiwan Strait.

To further complicate matters, there is no question that improvements in Chinese military technology and capabilities have altered the deterrence equation. Now, more than ever, China poses a serious military challenge to the United States when it comes to a conflict over Taiwan. Over the past decade, China has developed significant anti-access denial capabilities in the form of ballistic and cruise missiles, a submarine force, information and space warfare capabilities, and good air defenses. In other words, Washington's ability to decisively project force into the strait in order to deny Chinese military objectives is severely hindered.

In addition, China has a modest but improving nuclear force, including submarine-launched nuclear weapons. As Kennedy demonstrated during the Cold War, Washington's overwhelming nuclear superiority may not figure into a president's calculus if the equation is, say, Taipei for Los Angeles.[45] Thus, while threats of intense violence—even the use of nuclear weapons—may have compelled China to back away from attacking Taiwan in the past, such threats may grow less credible if China continues to develop capabilities to engage in lower levels of coercion against Taiwan.

There is also uncertainty about the costs the Chinese leadership is willing to tolerate when it comes to Taiwan. From Washington's perspective, it may not make much sense for China to engage in a conflict that might lead to severe economic dislocation. But from Beijing's vantage point, the costs may indeed be worthwhile if they prevent the drift of Taiwan from its orbit, result in the West forcing Taipei into some accommodation with Beijing, and reaffirm the legitimacy of the CCP's hold on the reigns of power by stamping it as the defender of "greater China."

Finally, deterring China is made more difficult by the fact that Chinese strategists—old and new—write regularly about how the "weaker" can defeat the "stronger."[46] While the conventional balance of forces will undoubtedly matter in the Chinese leadership's calculations of whether a conflict is worthwhile, that balance may not matter as much as we think. As noted above, history is replete with examples of advisors convincing their leadership that through the use of surprise and clever stratagems the power imbalance can be overcome. Deterring a power that believes it can be a David to your Goliath is no easy task.

That is not to say, however, that the U.S. lacks ways to improve its current deterrence posture. From a military point of view, a diversification of bases and access points for the U.S. military into the region is important in making China less confident that it can deny entry to U.S. forces from Japan or the Western Pacific. In a similar vein, the survivability of forward-deployed forces could be improved with better dispersal and air and missile defense capabilities. Improving the U.S. arsenal of long-range strike capabilities, and intelligence and surveillance assets, would help send the message that Beijing cannot use its massive strategic depth to launch land-based missiles with impunity.

It is also essential that the U.S. build up its intelligence capabilities with respect to China's military. As things stand, we know too little about what systems are being developed or how the Chinese intend to deploy them. Equally important, American intelligence and warning (I&W) must be substantially bolstered in order to make surprises less likely. Once in place, Washington must subtly convey to Beijing that military plans that depend on surprise for success are really not tenable given our intelligence and sensor capabilities.

There are other deterrence strategies potentially available to the United States and Taiwan as well. Taipei could embrace and Washington could support a "Swiss option" when it comes to defending Taiwan. As Barry Posen has described it,

> The army and the air force are deliberately structured so as to make the price of action very high. It is of critical importance not only that the initial defense be stalwart but also that painful and determined resistance continue over an extended period. The Swiss cannot deny their country to an adversary, but they

can make him pay for the privilege of entry, and punish him for staying around.[47]

Taiwan has similar options. It cannot deny with certainty a larger and better-armed military from initiating a conflict. It can, however, deny China its political objectives. This is especially true if China anticipates a quick fight or expects that a crushing blow will deliver Taiwan. For example, if Taiwan had thousands of well-trained marksmen, saboteurs, and special operators who could inflict protracted damage on Chinese invaders, Beijing might think twice about attacking the island. Taiwan's ongoing efforts to improve homeland defense and its ability to sustain a prolonged crisis can and should be accelerated to include measures to harden critical infrastructure and improve continuity of government procedures. In particular, it would be in Taiwan's interest to utilize its global leadership in high-tech know-how to develop the most up-to-date surveillance and warning assets that it can and increase the survivability of its civilian and military communications networks.

Taiwan could also take a page out of China's own asymmetric and anti-access strategy book, and let it be known that it intends to employ cost-imposing strategies as well. For example, once war has started, Taiwanese snipers and covert operators could be placed on the mainland to wreak havoc and threaten leadership targets. In addition, rather than try to match China's own naval buildup by buying increasingly expensive but vulnerable capital ships, Taiwan could spend its money on developing better undersea warfare capabilities, making the strait and the seas around Taiwan a far more contested area should a conflict arise.

Conclusion

It has been argued that the American deterrent vis à vis China is in good order precisely because Beijing understands its military inferiority, is satisfied with the status quo, and has no doubts about America's willingness to fight. As with the Cold War, Washington should be confident that no great power conflict is likely as long as it manages relations with Beijing competently.

However, as we have seen, the lessons of the Cold War are not as clear as they at first appear. Moreover, neither China's martial history nor its current strategic thinking should encourage undue confidence about Beijing having accepted a position of mutual deterrence. Certainly, China is not satisfied with the long-standing impasse over Taiwan—and, presumably, it will be even less so if the Taiwanese mark out a path independent of the mainland. And although the U.S. has repeatedly said it wants to see a peaceful resolution of cross-strait tensions, there is enough ambiguity in Washington's position that, under certain scenarios, one can imagine Beijing misreading Washington's own will to back up that policy.

Finally, perhaps the most immediate problem facing the United States' deterrence of China has less to do with China than with Washington's own policies. China's rapid and substantial military buildup has not been met in kind—either in the U.S. or Taiwan. The theory that, if the U.S. treats China as a competitor, it will become one is not buying either the U.S. or Taiwan the margin of safety that most presumed it would. While it is often said that we don't know what Chinese intentions are behind this buildup, this is misleading. In fact, we do know, because the Chinese have said time and again that they believe they must have the coercive capacity to prevent Taiwan from rejecting unification with the mainland and, if need be, to bend Taiwan to China's will. More recently, they have expressed the desire to have a military that matches up to China's new interests and roles on the global stage.[48] "Containing" China is not a realistic option. But if engaging China is to be the policy for the foreseeable future, it is imperative that the U.S. balance that policy with a hedging strategy that is at least as serious.

CHAPTER FOUR

JAPAN'S RESPONSE TO THE RISE OF CHINA

Back to the Future?

Michael R. Auslin

N o nation is as affected by—or as interested in—the rise of China as is Japan. Every aspect of Japan's national development, from culture to security, is influenced by what happens in China. This is, indeed, an old story, and in many ways the traditional pattern not only of Japanese history but of East Asia's as well. In this respect, China's rise unearths old fears, desires, and grievances, even as the new nature of Chinese power makes far more immediate its daily impact on Japan and its neighbors.

The Sino-Japanese relationship, however, is further complicated by an entirely new factor: for the first time in history, both Japan and China are world powers at the same moment. Previously, the tenor of their relationship was linked to the rise of one and the fall of the other—and policymakers on both sides seized every opportunity to shift the balance of power. Today, however, both are economic powerhouses with extensive international ties and the military strength of great powers. Never before have Tokyo and Beijing had to manage their relationship under such conditions, and it is clear that both are searching for equilibrium and advantage at the same time. The uniqueness of their current situation, however, is framed by the potential incompatibility of their indispensable economic relationship with their widely divergent political and security goals.

To understand the scope of Japan's response to China's rise, as well as its spillover into American global policy, this essay will first review the historical sweep of Sino-Japanese relations and then examine the impact of China's rise on Japanese economic and security doctrine, before concluding with an appraisal of the American role in the Beijing-Tokyo relationship.

Where the Sun Sets and Rises

Every aspect of Japan's history is intricately linked to that of China. Indeed, the very existence of Japan as a unified, advanced ethnic polity is due in no small measure to China's influence. From writing systems to cosmological beliefs, Japan's earliest tribal rulers looked to their giant western neighbor for imports that would allow them to solidify their power. After the introduction of Buddhism to Japan in the mid-6th century, Japanese rulers entered the regional Chinese ecumene. The flow of goods, ideas, and peoples continued between the two civilizations for centuries, facilitating vibrant exchange and, ultimately, competition.

One dynamic of Sino-Japanese history that has evolved and replayed itself over the centuries is the role of Chinese domestic politics in the greater region. Historically, instability within China and the northeast Asian region has directly affected Japanese security and policymaking. The collapse of various Chinese dynasties—from the Han through the Ming and Qing—which resulted in strife and warfare on the continent, brought waves of Chinese migrants to Japan, often instigating Japanese intervention. As early as the 7th century AD, for example, the Korean peninsula became the fulcrum of strategic interest in Japan, leading to a Japanese invasion that was eventually crushed by a Chinese counterforce. Fears of Chinese counterattacks on Japan planted the seeds for a century-long effort on the part of Japanese elites to forge a more centralized administration over the main islands. A similar dynamic replayed itself in the 19th century, as the then-feudal Japanese state sought to modernize itself in the face of a Western presence that had invaded China, opening the question of control over Korea. China's instability and Japan's desire to gain influence in Korea again drove Japanese forces into battle, occasioning a half-century struggle for mastery over Asia.[1]

Strategic concerns, however, were not the only sphere of Sino-Japanese relations. Of primary importance was Japan's participation in the so-called Chinese world order, especially in the trading networks that spread from southern Asia through the northeast. This great web, centered in the southern coastal region of China, linked numerous tribal regions and polities, facilitating between them a constant flow of goods. Much of what is today considered uniquely "Japanese"—green tea, soy sauce, and tatami matting, for example —first reached the islands' shores through this intricate trade network. In time, Japanese rulers established monopolies over the region's trade and used the resulting largesse to solidify their hold on power.

Japan's participation in the broader Chinese ecumene caused Japanese leaders to think differently about China. As early as the late 7th century, the famous Prince Shotoku—at that time little more than the co-leader of Japan's leading clan—addressed a missive to the Tang emperor with the salutation, "The Son of Heaven of the land where the sun rises sends this letter to the Son of Heaven of the land where the sun sets."[2] This Japanese desire to treat China as an equal shaped much of Japan's politics and policies. Successive dynastic collapses in China gradually led to a sense of superiority among the Japanese, who saw in their imperial family, as a common refrain went, "a dynastic line unbroken for ten thousand generations." It was this sense of superiority, even though tempered by an awe of China, that led Japan's modernizing rulers to challenge a weakened Beijing over control of Korea in 1894. Tokyo's ensuing victory in the Sino-Japanese War cemented in the minds of many Japanese the image of China as a divided and backward country. China's continuing political fragmentation in the 1920s and 1930s convinced the ultramilitarist leaders of Japan's army that the country was ripe for the picking. Indeed, the rapacity of the Japanese invasion in 1937 can be explained in part by Japan's long-standing sense of superiority over China. More than six decades after the end of World War II, the traumatic memories of the war continue to trouble Sino-Japanese relations.

The Fruits of Chinese Growth

For the first decades after World War II, both China and Japan focused on their respective domestic crises. Japan's rebuilding process after the devastation of the war was correlated to the U.S. occupation from 1945 to 1952 and eventually led to the bilateral security alliance between the U.S. and Japan. Throughout the 1950s and 1960s, Tokyo concentrated its efforts on economic recovery. Prime Minister Yoshida Shigeru's Liberal Democratic Party, which held power uninterruptedly from 1955 through 1993, particularly emphasized export-led growth. And indeed, by the 1980s, Japan was one of the world's leading producers of consumer-oriented items, as well as ships, heavy machinery, and the like. It ran massive current account surpluses and began to invest heavily in overseas property.

In contrast, China's post-war descent into civil war, followed by the victory of Mao Zedong's Chinese Communist Party (CCP), meant that relations between China and Japan were all but non-existent throughout the later 1940s and 1950s. By the 1970s, however, Chinese leader Deng Xiaoping began easing CCP control over the mainland's economy, setting up special economic zones, and instituting gradual market-oriented mechanisms. Within a decade, China was posting double-digit domestic growth, and by 2000 was rapidly becoming one of the world's largest exporters of medium- and low-end consumer goods. In the space of just 25 years, China's trade with the United States, for example, skyrocketed from just $5 billion in 1980 to more than $340 billion in 2006.[3] Just as China's economy was really beginning to take off, however, the Japanese economy, shaken by the 1989 collapse of the property-value and asset-price bubble, entered a decade-and-a-half slump, weighed down by bad debt, stifling government regulation, and inefficient industries.

China's economic growth poses a unique set of challenges for Japan, which must balance the loss of market share to China with ever-deepening trade relations with its neighbor to the West. Throughout the 1990s and early 2000s, Tokyo quickly moved to expand trade with China; by 2006, China was Japan's largest overall trade partner, with Japan importing more from China than from any other country, and exporting more to China than any country save the United States. Year-on-year growth averaged 20 percent from 2003 to 2005, and total bilateral trade between the two countries topped $200 billion in 2006.[4]

By 2000, as Japan was beginning to tackle long-needed reforms in government regulation, clean up bad debt, and modernize inefficient industry sectors, the Chinese market had become vital to the country's economic recovery. Japanese exports to China more than doubled from $30.4 billion in 2000 to $80.3 billion in 2005.[5] More importantly, nearly every export sector saw a doubling or more—chemical and non-electric machinery exports, for example, more than tripled, while electrical equipment and metals exports doubled.

Japan further responded to China's economic rise by taking advantage of cheaper labor costs on the mainland. Leading Japanese companies such as Nintendo and Sony licensed out the production of consumer electronic goods to China, while Toyota began producing some of its models, including the popular Prius, in partnership with Chinese firms.[6] Beijing's willingness to allow foreign enterprises to operate on Chinese soil translated into Japanese firms directly employing one million Chinese and indirectly employing more than 9 million through subcontracts with mainland companies.[7] In roughly the same period, Japanese annual foreign direct investment in China more than quadrupled, from just over $1 billion in 2000 to $4.5 billion in 2004. In all, Japan invested more than $28 billion in China from 1992 through 2004.[8]

Japanese consumers also benefited from China's rise. Take Uniqlo for example: The Japanese clothing retailer purchased more than 90 percent of its products from Chinese sources, allowing it to emerge as a major low-cost seller. Textiles as a whole accounted for nearly 20 percent of Chinese exports to Japan, while foodstuffs accounted for just over 7 percent.[9] The result was a burgeoning of lower-cost consumer goods for Japanese, who throughout the 1990s and early 2000s were struggling with flat personal income growth and a falling savings rate.

In sum, China's economic rise meant a boom in bilateral trade, just at the time when the Japanese economic miracle, which for three decades had propelled the country to the first rank of industrialized nations, was sputtering. China's thirst for capital and goods helped to pull Japan out of its economic doldrums. Not surprisingly, Japanese bureaucrats and businessmen remain eager to expand trade relations and hope to eventually sign a free-trade agreement (FTA) between the two countries. Interestingly, the largest growth in trade occurred precisely when political relations between Japan and China were at their lowest ebb and Japanese fears of China's growing military strength were becoming more pronounced.

Fears of Chinese Strength

China's economic rise, as well as the rapid strengthening of its military and its newfound prominence on the world stage, is actually returning East Asia to a traditional posture.[10] For centuries, China dominated the region—its culture spreading out in all directions, its major cities a magnet for foreign legations and traders, and its rulers demanding obeisance from representatives of far-flung polities. Its military forces, too, ventured as far west as Central Asia and throughout the eastern continental range, while in the 15th century, its navy—under the command of the fabled Zheng He—voyaged as far as eastern Africa. Yet China's 19th-century fall from hegemony occurred precisely as the international system was moving toward an increased recognition of sovereign nation-states. Not surprisingly, Beijing's attempts to reassert its traditional primacy often alarm its neighbors, whose long memories of Chinese dominance clash with the modern precepts of sovereignty, not to mention the lived experience of independence.

Among the nations of Asia, Japan occupies a unique position in relation to China. It was, of course, the first of the Asian states to consciously modernize itself, creating its own empire and contending with the European powers for mastery over Asia. More pertinently, Japan directly challenged Chinese hegemony, defeating it in 1895 for control over Korea and invading and occupying northern and coastal China during the 1930s and early 1940s. Throughout the post-war period, Japan's military alliance with the United States insulated the country from any sense of threat from China, even as Tokyo and Beijing normalized political relations in 1972.

While Tokyo has worried about being diplomatically bested by Beijing, its more proximate concern is the rapid expansion and modernization of Chinese military forces over the past decade. Although the People's Liberation Army (PLA) downsized twice in the past decade, cutting 700,000 troops to reach a base of 2.3 million men in arms, it still dwarfs the Japan Self-Defense Force (JSDF) total of 240,000.[11] Of greater importance is the PLA's growing budget, which for more than ten years has registered annual double-digit increases. China announced that its 2007 budget would increase by 17.8 percent, officially totaling $45 billion; the U.S. Defense Intelligence Agency, however, estimates that the true number could be as high as $85 billion to $125 billion, which would make China the world's second-biggest military spender, and the largest in Asia.[12]

China's military modernization has, in the space of a decade, turned an outdated force into a contender for regional supremacy. Indeed, the advances in China's missile, air, and naval forces have the potential to directly threaten Japanese security, regardless of the strength of the American security guarantee under the U.S.-Japan alliance. Thus Japan now perceives its largest neighbor—and traditional competitor in the region—as a palpable military threat.

How Tokyo handles this threat is shaped—at least for now—by two factors that have shaped Japanese military doctrine since 1952. First, the military alliance with the United States provides an ultimate security guarantee—backed up by tens of thousands of U.S. troops stationed in Japan and by an implicit promise to use nuclear weapons to protect Japan, if necessary. Second, the restrictions on the use of force enshrined in Article 9 of Japan's postwar constitution keep ambiguous the actual legal range of options open to Tokyo. As a result, Japanese military forces today remain defensively oriented—Japan has no missile forces, no long-range bombers or attack fighters, no ballistic missile submarines, and no amphibious landing vessels.

But China's decade-long military buildup particularly threatens Japan's sea-lanes of communication (SLOCs) and airspace. As an island nation, Japan is dependent on free passage through the seas—it imports all of its oil, 80 percent of which comes through the Malacca Straits. Its exports and imports of food and raw materials are similarly sea-based. With a limited number of choke points separating Japan from major SLOCs—particularly in the south, at the Sea of China, and in the north, near the Straits of Okhotsk—effective control of these vital points during a conflict is a prerequisite for any successful defensive strategy.

Thus, the growth in China's naval forces, combined with its strategic goal of gaining a blue-water navy, is inherently troublesome to Japan. Japan's Maritime Self-Defense Force (JMSDF) currently has a total of 151 ships, including 53 destroyers and 16 submarines.[13] These forces are, of course, buttressed by the U.S. Seventh Fleet, which included the USS *Kitty Hawk* battle group and nine guided-missile destroyers, including several Aegis-class warships.[14] The Chinese navy, on the other hand, has a total of 260 vessels and has been aggressively adding new destroyers, new submarines, and new naval air assets to its fleet.

In November 2004, a Chinese nuclear-powered submarine entered Japanese territorial waters, occasioning a brief pursuit by Japanese coast guard ships. This and other unspecified incidents of Chinese vessels engaging in "some exercises or intelligence collections" near Japan's waters receive specific attention in Tokyo's defense white papers, indicating the degree of seriousness with which officials take these displays of new Chinese naval capabilities.[15]

Of equal, if less acknowledged, concern is the growth in Chinese missile and air capabilities. Since the mid-1990s, the PLA has invested heavily in modernizing its ballistic-missile capabilities— and Tokyo has noted in its annual defense white papers that Beijing is attempting to develop mobile, solid-fuel ICBMs and submarine-launched ballistic missiles (SLBMs).[16] More pertinently, Beijing deploys hundreds of intermediate-range ballistic missiles (IRBMs) and medium-range ballistic missiles (MRBMs) that can reach Japan as well as other countries in East Asia. Although the majority of those missiles target Taiwan, they could easily be retargeted in a crisis between China and Japan. Complementing the missile forces are the more than 100 medium-range H-6 bombers, which, while based on an early Soviet bomber design, have been upgraded to carry modern attack cruise missiles and conduct all-weather, day-night counter-maritime missions.

Also causing anxiety in Tokyo is China's growing capability in space, which is marked not only by the success of its lunar program but, more directly, its successful anti-satellite (ASAT) test in the beginning of 2007. While the unannounced test immediately increased international suspicion of China's growing military capabilities, the ASAT test was of particular concern to Japan, which has only three working spy satellites in orbit and no immediate plans to launch any more. Should China continue to perfect its ASAT capabilities, Japan's small number of observation satellites would quickly become easy targets, thus reducing not only Tokyo's ability to monitor Chinese activities, but also its information-sharing capabilities with U.S. forces stationed in Japan.

In response to China's growing military power, Japanese civilian and defense planners have begun to move past longstanding postures. Former Prime Minister Junichiro Koizumi expanded the scope and powers of the Prime Minister's Office (*Kantei*) during his 2001–2006 term. Security issues were also the focus of his short-lived successor in office, Shinzo Abe. One of Abe's initiatives in his first cabinet was to explore the possibility of establishing a Japanese National Security Council (JNSC) to replace the current ad-hoc Security Council of Japan. The JNSC would include a Special Advisor and Secretariat, and would expand its scope to "include basic diplomatic and defense policies for enhancing Japan's national security."[17] Along the same lines, in 2007, Japan's Defense Agency (JDA) was renamed the Ministry of Defense and elevated to cabinet-level status.

In addition to centralizing its security decision-making, Tokyo has moved to upgrade its intelligence-gathering capabilities, including the previously mentioned spy satellites. The impetus for such moves comes in equal measure from concern over China's growth and the threat of North Korea's missile and nuclear programs. Joint intelligence sharing with the United States, in particular, remains a top priority for the Japanese; recent ministerial-level talks with the United States have stressed real-time collection, analysis, and dissemination of intelligence crucial to both parties. Such reforms are not limited to operational intelligence activities for Japan's Self-Defense Force, but are taking place at the national level as well. As prime minister, for example, Abe established a study group to explore greater centralization of intelligence activities in the *Kantei*, though the process is still in the early stages.

Officially, however, Japan's "Basis of Defense Policy" has not changed. The government continues to adhere to long-standing declarations, including that of having an "exclusively defense-oriented policy," "not becoming a military power," maintaining the "three non-nuclear principles," and "ensuring civilian control."[18] But, at the same time, as outlined in its 2004 *National Defense Program Outline,* Japan has begun to broaden its vision of what constitutes "security" to include more than simply homeland defense. And while the "first objective of Japan's security policy is to prevent any threat from reaching Japan," "the second objective is to improve the international security environment in order to prevent any threat from reaching Japan." Facing a "new security environment," Japan's defense capabilities would have to be improved to handle not only a threat to Japan proper but also international terrorism, proliferation, the security of maritime traffic, and, most importantly, the potential threats found "in Japan's neighborhood." [19]

Accordingly, Japan is slowly beginning to strengthen key capabilities, particularly those leveraging high technology for force-multiplying purposes. While defense spending remained relatively flat during the past half decade, Tokyo's 2007–2008 defense budget reversed that trend, indicating a desire to begin offsetting Chinese strengths in certain areas. The 1.5 percent overall increase in the 2007–2008 budget stresses anti-missile technology, one of Japan's areas of greatest focus in recent years. Japan has joined the United States in developing ballistic missile defense systems and projects spending nearly $2 billion on missile defense in the coming years.

Similarly, Japan is moving to upgrade its air capabilities in ways that will move it closer to having defensive as well as offensive capabilities. The backbone of the Air Self-Defense Force (ASDF) is currently the Mitsubishi-licensed F-15 J/DJ fighter, of which the ASDF operates approximately 220.[20] Along with nearly 90 domestically produced smaller F-2 fighters, the ASDF fields more than 300 fighter jets, supplemented by AWACs E-2C. Given the necessity of defending Japan's extended airspace, the ASDF is moving to incorporate new mission-extending technologies.

A major priority for the ASDF has been to gain in-flight refueling capabilities. To this end, Japan has purchased four modified KC-767 tankers from the Boeing Corporation. Japan began to take delivery of the tankers in 2008 and hopes to have them fully operational by 2010.[21] The ASDF claims that it needs refueling capabilities to allow fighters to stay on patrol longer, but the tankers could also be used for longer-flight missions, such as to North Korea or the continent.

A higher-profile goal of the ASDF, however, is the F-X support fighter project, which aims to replace Japan's aging F-15s and F-2s. As part of this project, Tokyo is looking to purchase a fifth-generation fighter and has considered the F-35 Joint Strike Fighter, and also expressed interest in the F-22 Raptor.[22] Although initially rebuffed in 2007 by the U.S. on the possible purchase or co-production of the F-22, Japan still sees the Raptor as its fighter of choice, and it is likely Tokyo will renew its request. Regardless of the outcome, however, the Ministry of Defense and the ASDF have made clear their desire to significantly upgrade their defensive and long-range capabilities, thereby offsetting China's continued increase in air power.

In addition to these unilateral moves, Japan has begun to participate in regional security exercises, most recently joining the United States, India, Australia, and Singapore in a massive joint activity in September 2007 in the Bay of Bengal. Exercise Malabar 07-2 included two U.S. carrier strike groups, more than 20 additional ships, and 20,000 sailors from the five participating countries. The exercises were interpreted by many as a clear sign of regional concern over the growth of China's naval power, and as a nascent response to China's military cooperation with the nations of the Shanghai Cooperation Organization (SCO).

A New Asian Geopolitical Competition

But it is not only in the military sphere that Japan is rethinking its global posture. Tokyo is increasingly approaching regional and even international politics as a field of competition, even as it labors to maintain its economic relationship with China. Indeed, the belief that Asia's future is being shaped in the various multilateral forums and through bilateral free-trade agreements has spurred the beginning of a new diplomatic and strategic outreach on the part of Tokyo.

Since World War II, Asia has lacked a NATO- or EU-type multilateral structure. This has meant primarily bilateral and ad-hoc responses to regional issues. This trend was reified by the hub-and-spoke nature of the U.S. alliances with Japan, South Korea, and Australia, which did not evolve into a larger multi-polar alliance system. Pan-regional security and political discussions, however, have dramatically increased since 1994, when the 10-member ASEAN group formed an ancillary organization, the ASEAN Regional Forum, seeking to forge indigenous approaches to transnational problems. These efforts are still only beginning, but China and Japan already see them as open fields for diplomatic competition.

Indeed, nimble Chinese diplomacy has given Beijing a major presence in ASEAN-sponsored initiatives, such as ASEAN Plus Three (which includes China, Japan, and South Korea). In November 2002, for example, China's then-Premier Zhu Rongji signed an FTA with ASEAN, slated to begin in 2010, which will link 1.7 billion people with a combined GDP of nearly $3 trillion. Closer economic ties between China and ASEAN nations are likely to translate into closer political relations, potentially reducing Japan's influence in the region. Any diminution of its role in the region would be of serious concern to Japan, for Southeast Asia is not only an important market for Japanese exports but also home to the world's key shipping lanes.

Beijing has supplemented its outreach with the creation of its own multilateral forum, the Shanghai Cooperation Organization. Established in 2001, the SCO brings together China, Kazakhstan, Kyrgyzstan, Russia, Tajikistan, and Uzbekistan.[23] This organization of non-democratic states with vast natural energy resources will undoubtedly have very different approaches to development issues, free markets, human rights abuses, democratization, and the like than the traditional Western alliances. Its influence could expand beyond Central Asia to the Pacific region, especially as energy-thirsty nations in East and Southeast Asia look to SCO members for resources. In August 2007, the members of the SCO engaged in a war game exercise, further stoking regional concern over the group's long-range objectives.

In response, Japan has often been perceived as playing catch-up, tardily responding to China's diplomatic initiatives. Nonetheless, Tokyo has steadily pursued a two-tiered diplomatic track, making its own overtures to targets of Chinese attention, such as ASEAN, while simultaneously seeking to bring together the Asia-Pacific's major democracies.

Inevitably, Japan's initiatives have caused tension in the Sino-Japanese relationship. During the majority of the post-war period, Tokyo scrupulously avoided the appearance of interfering in what China considered to be its internal affairs. In 1972, Japan went so far as to break diplomatic relations with Taiwan as part of its normalization with Beijing. The growth of Sino-Japanese antagonism during the late 1990s and early 2000s, however, along with the concurrent deepening of the U.S.-Japan relationship, slowly pushed Tokyo into more explicit positions regarding regional security and the larger democracy project. This was revealed most clearly in February 2005, when the Joint Statement of the U.S.-Japan Security Consultative Committee (SCC) included a line saying that the two allies would "encourage the peaceful resolution of issues concerning the Taiwan Strait through dialogue."[24]

Since the SCC was the highest ministerial-level meeting of the alliance partners, including the secretaries of state and defense and the ministers of foreign affairs and defense, Beijing considered the statement a direct challenge to its claim over Taiwan. Beijing's response was to sternly tell the U.S. and Japan to stay out of China's internal affairs, further adding to the strain on Sino-Japanese relations. Nevertheless, Japan slowly and discreetly has drawn closer to Taiwan during the first decade of the 21st century. Japanese lawmakers meet regularly to discuss Taiwan security issues, former Taiwan president Lee Teng-hui has visited Japan twice, and people-to-people exchanges between Taiwan and Japan have expanded.[25] Chinese belligerence over Taiwan's independence had a ripple effect on Japan, which saw it as a potential harbinger of Chinese dominance in the region, especially after Beijing passed the Anti-Secession Law in March 2005 in the wake of the Joint SCC statement.[26]

Japan, like China, has also undertaken new regional initiatives. Tokyo's major initiative with ASEAN was to attempt to push the nascent East Asia Summit (EAS) to include more democratic states. ASEAN conceived of the EAS as the first true pan-Asian forum in which economic, political, and ultimately security issues would be addressed. The initial membership was slated to be identical to the ASEAN Plus Three grouping, but before the first meeting in December 2005, Japan and a few of the ASEAN states, notably Singapore, pushed to include India, Australia, and New Zealand as charter members. The move was seen as a potential check on the influence of China and as an attempt by Japan to include a values-based orientation—one that might include statements on democratization, rule of law, and human rights—in EAS pronouncements. China resisted the inclusion of India in particular, but was ultimately forced to accept it.

Successful in bringing more democracies into the EAS, Tokyo then sought to leapfrog China's FTA agreement with ASEAN. At the ASEAN economic ministers' meeting in April 2006, then-Finance Minister Toshihiro Nikai unveiled the "Comprehensive Economic Partnership for East Asia" (CEPEA), a $100 million initiative to create an East Asian Organization for Economic Cooperation and Development (OECD). Both India and South Korea indicated support for the idea, which would establish study groups to explore the feasibility of establishing a common currency and/or an East Asian FTA agreement. Clearly, any such proposal would take decades to achieve, but Tokyo appeared primarily interested in driving the process of political and economic integration in Asia, thereby diluting China's influence in the region.

At the same time, Tokyo sought to more directly leverage its position as a mature democratic state by increasingly linking itself with the United States, India, and Australia. And indeed, in March 2007, Japan and Australia signed a new defense agreement, expanding security ties between the two countries. More expansively, then-Prime Minister Abe, building on his predecessor's outreach to the U.S., India, and Australia, called for an enhanced quadrilateral relationship

—an "arc of freedom"— that would have served as a nascent alliance among the four democracies. Although the proposal—put forward in a visit to India in August 2007—lacked specifics, it clearly was an attempt to frame the question of Asia's future as one of democracy versus authoritarianism. The response to Abe's call was muted, as none of the major players wanted to antagonize China. But the idea itself is likely to reemerge in the future, especially if regional tensions over economic and security issues continue to grow.

The Sino-American-Japanese Triangle

As detailed above, China's rise has challenged Japan to reconsider a larger grand strategy—not only in Asia, but also globally. The interconnections of politics, economics, and security requirements have become increasingly clear, much in the way they were immediately after World War II, when Japan faced the tremendous necessity of rebuilding its shattered economy while at the same time being threatened by both the Soviet Union and Communist China. Threads of the current debate have been spinning out for several years, but so far no overarching, comprehensive articulation of Japan's strategy has emerged. Both prime ministers Koizumi and Abe shared a vision of a Japan more engaged with the international community and playing a role that befitted a great power. With their passing from the scene, Japan's leaders will likely tone down such bold rhetoric. Smoothing relations with the whole of Asia will no doubt rise in priority. That said, the issues raised by China's rise will continue to push Japan slowly but probably inexorably in the geostrategic direction set out by Abe and Koizumi.

For the foreseeable future, the bedrock of Japanese security policy remains the alliance with the United States. The insurance this alliance provides has indeed become more important due to China's rise. The particular capabilities the Japanese seek to gain are also most effective within the larger alliance structure. Likewise, Washington will find it very difficult, if not impossible, to maintain its position in Asia without its Japanese partner. America's outreach to new allies, access to new bases, regional economic liberalization, and military-to-military relationships are necessary and prudent moves, but nothing on the horizon is capable of substituting for the Japanese alliance.

The most prudent course of action for the United States is therefore to maintain its close relationship with Japan and further strengthen the alliance. Washington has a key role to play in nurturing the evolution of Japan's national security apparatus. Japanese concerns about China are only likely to rise in the coming years. With major resource constraints on the country's defense budget, Japanese policymakers and defense officials will have to focus on force-multiplying technologies and leveraging current capabilities. Greater interoperability with U.S. forces is one important approach, and a deeper research and development relationship may well benefit long-range Japanese planning. Washington, however, will have to be realistic about the degree to which Japan can continue to participate in ballistic-missile defense research, as the high expense of such participation constrains resources required for force modernization.

Similarly, the U.S. should support Japan's attempts to maintain its influence in regional multilateral forums. While such arrangements are highly unlikely to turn into full-fledged political mechanisms anytime soon, it would be detrimental to Japan's interests to be isolated from such developments or to cede primacy to China in influencing these groups. Tokyo must be perceived as a central actor in the region if it is to remain one. Where the U.S. is a member of such forums, as in the Asia-Pacific Economic Cooperation or the ASEAN Regional Forum, it should work with Japan to support democratically oriented proposals. This will, in turn, create the conditions for other democratic states to form a community of interests. In forums where Washington is not a member, as in the East Asia Summit, it should be in close contact with Tokyo and work to support Japan's outreach to nations in the region.

Such an approach is not designed to contain China, although Beijing will have considerable interest in suggesting that it is. Rather, it is part of a crucial policy of bolstering Asia's strongest and most important democracy, and providing a robust vision of international norms and interests that should be a priority in the region. Japan and China will continue to have one of the world's most complex, and delicate, relationships—they will, for the coming decades, be both economic partners and political rivals.

To China's consternation, its rapid rise has not been matched, as expected, by Japan's continued decline. Instead, we are entering a period of unchartered waters for both Japan and China—and, as such, for the United States as well. But, ultimately, if China's rise to great power status is to be relatively benign, it will be because the U.S. and Japan have together helped create a regional economic, diplomatic, and strategic environment that induces China to move in positive directions and not down avenues that lead to greater competition and fear. U.S.-Japan ties must be the cornerstone of that strategy, even while both countries continue to engage China as best they can.

CHAPTER FIVE

FACING REALITIES

Multilateralism for the Asia-Pacific Century

Gary J. Schmitt

M ore people live under democratic rule in Asia than in any other place on the globe. Asia is also home to the two fastest rising powers in the world, India and China. Yet neither America's system of alliances nor the region's multilateral organizations suffi- ciently account for these new realities.

In 1980, of the major countries in East Asia, South Asia, and the Asia-Pacific region, only five countries—Japan, India, Sri Lanka, New Zealand, and Australia—could be described as democratic and free. The total population of those five states was just short of 900 million. To that list, today one can add: Indonesia, South Korea, Mongolia, Pakistan, the Philippines, Thailand, Nepal, East Timor, Malaysia, and Taiwan, with almost 2 billion people living under democratic (if not always perfect) rule. In Europe—now largely "whole and free," and the traditional focus of most U.S. alliance statecraft—that figure is about one-third as big.

China and India are in some respects just returning to the former prominence they once held in economic affairs. At the beginning of the 1700s, China, Europe, and India each accounted for approximately 25 percent of the world's economic output. By the 1900s, Europe and the United States made up more than 50 percent of the world economy, with China and India each contributing less than 10 percent of the world's total. As a result of reforms undertaken in China since 1978 and in India since 1991, both countries now look increasingly set to return to their place of prominence. Since the late 1970s, China has enjoyed an economic growth rate of more than 9 percent per year, while India saw its GDP grow by an average of 5.5 percent in the 1990s and from 7 percent to 9 percent this decade. Even though their per capita incomes are still far below the world's other major economies, China and India, through the sheer size of their populations, are increasingly important economic players. If current trends continue, first China will overtake five of the G-6 countries—namely Italy, France, the UK, Germany, and Japan—in the immediate years ahead, and then India will do the same over the next two decades. Again, if projections hold, China's GDP will obtain parity with the United States sometime in this century's third decade, and India will reach that status a few years later.

But economies and populations are not the only ways in which these two emerging powerhouses are growing: equally impressive is their growth and investment in high-end technologies and expanding military capabilities. China's declared defense budget has seen double-digit increases for nearly two decades, approaching 18 percent in the past two years. Similarly, India's military expenditures (in rupees) have more than quintupled since the early 1990s, and (in constant U.S. dollars) have essentially doubled over the past decade. Both India and China are rising, and rising fast. As the National Intelligence Council has pointedly noted, "The likely emergence of China and India as new major global players—similar to the rise of Germany in the 19th century and the United States in the early 20th century—will transform the geopolitical landscape, with the impacts potentially as dramatic as those of the previous two centuries."[1]

The common perception is that Washington has done very little in response to these significant changes in the Asian strategic landscape. On the face of things, that perception is supported by the fact that the core of the American security effort in Asia still rests on the "hub and spoke" system of bilateral treaties (with Japan, South Korea, and Australia) that has been in place since the early years of the Cold War. Moreover, while there has been a proliferation of multilateral institutions in the region—the Association of Southeast Asian Nations (ASEAN), the ASEAN Regional Forum, ASEAN Plus Three (APT), the East Asia Summit, the Shanghai Cooperation Organization (SCO), the Asia-Pacific Economic Cooperation (APEC) and the so-called "Six Party Talks"—the U.S. plays an active role in only the last two, with the former limited to economic affairs and the latter an ad hoc arrangement among northeast Asian powers whose purpose is to address the North Korean nuclear problem.[2] On the whole—and apart from an occasional statement by the last two presidents on their vision for a "fellowship" of Asian democracies—the U.S. has been reluctant to rethink its system of treaty relations or reexamine what multilateral organizations might best suit the changed Asian strategic environment.[3]

This is not to say that the U.S. has been entirely passive in the face of these changes. The Bush Administration, in particular, has set about strengthening ties with key allies, most notably Japan and Australia. This has meant working more closely with Tokyo and Canberra on a bilateral level, while also conducting joint ministerial meetings among the three capitals and trying to create a new consultative relationship with NATO for our Asia-Pacific allies. Washington has also begun, in the face of the continued expansion of and improvement in Chinese military capabilities, to increase its own air and sea forces in the region and increase military-to-military ties with a number of states in the region. And, as Daniel Twining has argued, the U.S. has undertaken a subtle but concerted effort to improve strategic ties with India, Indonesia, and Vietnam, with the goal of "facilitating the ascent of friendly Asian centers of power that will both constrain any Chinese bid for hegemony and allow the United States to retain its position as Asia's decisive strategic actor."[4]

So, while it is true that Washington has not been idly sitting on its hands in the face of Asia's strategic evolution, it is also true that America is still largely operating off of its Cold War "hub and spoke" system and that whatever innovative steps it has taken remain basically consultative, lacking formal institutional support. Whether this approach is adequate is the question this chapter will try to answer.

At a minimum, the current strategy assumes that over the long run the vicissitudes of international politics in Asia are such that there is no need to ground these less formal measures in a concrete set of arrangements. In short, if left to be, the general trends in Asia will result in a regional set of power relationships in which American interests are met without Washington having to do much of anything. Yet, as Washington and states in the region have already noted, immediate concerns—be it the war on terror or the problem of North Korea's nuclear-weapons program—have a way of forcing to the back burner longer-term strategic initiatives, such as creating a community of like-minded democratic states in the region. Moreover, precisely because America's key allies in the region are democracies, there is no guarantee that today's level of cooperation will remain as changes in leadership occur (as Washington has witnessed in the case of South Korea, Japan, and Australia over the past decade). This is not to suggest that in such cases an ally stops acting as an ally but rather that there are opportunity costs for not institutionalizing such cooperation and facilitating an alliance's ability to better withstand the vicissitudes of domestic politics.

Multilateralism South and North

ASEAN

The oldest and most important multilateral forum in Asia is ASEAN, the Association of Southeast Asian Nations. Now comprising ten members (Brunei, Cambodia, Indonesia, Laos, Malaysia, Myanmar/Burma, the Philippines, Singapore, Thailand, and Vietnam), ASEAN celebrated its 40th anniversary in 2007. The forum was established at a time of considerable tension within the region as a result of the not-so-cold war in Indochina and ongoing territorial disputes among a number of states, and a key principle guiding its founding and subsequent activities was non-interference in the domestic affairs of other states. This principle was in the interest of the then-member governments, each of which was, at the time, ruled by autocrats of one form or another. ASEAN decision-making was, in turn, to be a product of unanimity among member states.

Although these principles undoubtedly helped stabilize the region and enabled it to progress economically, the hope that ASEAN would become something more has not become reality. This was exhibited most clearly in the run-up to the 2007 ASEAN annual summit. Prior to the summit, an "eminent persons" committee drafted a far-reaching "ASEAN Charter." Among the draft's more remarkable provisions was the statement that peace and stability in the region would now depend on "the active strengthening of democratic values, good governance, rejection of unconstitutional and undemocratic changes of government, the rule of law, including international humanitarian law, and respect for human rights and fundamental freedoms." The draft's authors also proposed modifying ASEAN's practice of decision-making by unanimous consensus.

The working assumption behind these provisions was that continued regional progress in the areas of economics and security would only be assured if member countries were governed democratically. The proposed charter, if adopted as drafted, would have the salutary effect of allowing newer democracies, such as Indonesia, to help create a regional norm that would further solidify their

95

own rule. At the same time, the charter's drafters recognized that new initiatives to harmonize economic and security policies across the region were unlikely to be implemented in fact by governments with radically different philosophies of governance. In brief, the goal of the new charter was to set in place something along the lines of the 1957 Treaty of Rome, the founding document of what eventually became the European Union.[5]

What the ASEAN members ultimately adopted at the summit fell short of that goal.[6] The charter, once ratified by member states, will strengthen ASEAN's own secretariat and the role of its secretary-general. It will also give ASEAN a "legal personality" under international law (which, in turn, will allow it to join the United Nations and receive ambassadors). However, the more forward-leaning elements of the proposed charter were largely set aside. Instead, the charter, as adopted, reaffirmed the principles of "non-interference" and decision-making by unanimous consensus, and provided no practical mechanism allowing ASEAN collectively to take a tough stance on issues such as human-rights violations or coups among members. Despite the high-minded rhetoric coming from ASEAN and its supporters about it laying the basis for an East Asian community, "the only fundamental principle of international society it has reinforced is a realist commitment to the inviolable sovereignty of the nation-state."[7] As Ralph Cossa acerbically notes, with its newly adopted charter, ASEAN now has a legal personality, "complete with its own flag, emblem, anthem . . . and motto: One Vision, One Identity, One Community. Now it is time to choose an official flower and an ASEAN bird. Might," he goes on to suggest, they pick "the shrinking violet and the ostrich, in keeping with ASEAN's continuing tendency to shrink away from dealing with sensitive issues while burying its head in the sand and pretending that regional problems will somehow go away?"[8]

The fact that ASEAN's charter ended up where it did is not surprising. When the Treaty of Rome was signed, all the signatory states were democracies and their security was grounded by membership in a U.S.-led NATO. ASEAN still reflects a mix of regimes (and will likely continue to for some time) and sees itself as involved in a very careful balancing act between an increasingly powerful China that resides in its backyard, and the super-powerful but distant and sometimes distracted United States.[9]

With respect to China, ASEAN's goal has been to avoid being locked into some sort of soft tributary relationship by creating a web of economic, cultural, and defense ties with Beijing. Having scared its neighbors by its aggressive stance on disputed territorial boundaries in the early 1990s, China has reversed course and signed on to a number of agreements designed to reassure the neighboring ASEAN states of its peaceful intentions. According to many Asian experts, China has become socialized internationally, adopting the values and norms of the so-called "ASEAN way."[10]

The question is, will such a strategy work over the long term? In the early 1990s, for example, China's GDP was roughly equal to that of all of the member states of ASEAN combined; today, China's GDP is more than twice that of ASEAN. Similarly, in the early 1990s, China's military was seen as backward, poorly equipped, and with only minimal power projection capabilities; today, after nearly two decades of reform and new procurements, China's military is beginning to look like that of a great power. And while it is said that "ASEAN can be expected to work harder at shoring itself up as an effective regional organization in order to better manage increasing interdependence with China,"[11] the issue is whether it has the institutional wherewithal or resources to do so adequately.

At the moment, it is not in China's interest to throw its weight around. (And, of course, what China loses in not throwing its weight around, it gains by ASEAN's principle of non-interference.) As Jones and Smith point out, in signing on to various non-binding agreements with ASEAN, China has committed "to very little." For the time being, the ASEAN Regional Forum's "preferred strategy of managing problems rather than solving them . . . serves China's rather than ASEAN's long-term strategic interest."[12] Moreover, if China's power grows as expected, won't the so-called "ASEAN way" open the door to (or, more specifically, keep it from being locked against) the region falling into the very subordinate relationship it would like to avoid? Tactically, with a consensus-first approach to addressing issues, ASEAN leaves itself open to China's having a virtual veto over new initiatives within the region by having friendly ASEAN members put a halt to any initiatives with which Beijing disagrees. Presumably, this is one reason—even if not explicitly stated—why some members of ASEAN, such as Indonesia and the Philippines, were in favor of including a more robust statement of liberal principles in the charter and changing the association's decision-making procedures.

The Six-Party Talks

Whatever the current and prospective problems with ASEAN may be, at least it can be said that Southeast Asia has an organization around which the states of the region can communicate with each other on a regular and sustained basis. The same cannot be said for Northeast Asia: there is no permanent institutional arrangement for that region.

Since the advent of the "Six-Party Talks" in the fall of 2003, however, there has been a steady drumbeat among area specialists for turning this forum (comprising the United States, Japan, South Korea, Russia, China, and North Korea, and specifically tasked with addressing North Korea's nuclear weapons program) into a more enduring structure, perhaps along the lines of the Organization for Security and Cooperation in Europe.[13] And, indeed, the Bush administration in its last year in office was exploring the idea of a Northeast Asia security forum as a follow-on to the talks as well.[14]

Certainly, there are plenty of issues for such a forum to address: a possible North Korean regime collapse, Korean unification, refugee flows, transparency in military affairs, and energy supplies, to name just a few. But whatever the potential merits of perpetuating the Six-Party Talks (or a modified five-party version that would exclude North Korea), the missing element right now is an agreed-on set of principles that would guide any such organization. It is useful to remember that the OSCE's predecessor, the Conference on Security and Cooperation in Europe (CSCE), was established on the basis of the Helsinki Final Act and included a lengthy list of declarations and texts covering issues as disparate as security, economics, science, the environment, and human rights. It's possible, of course, that a similar statement of principles could be adopted by five of the six Northeast Asian powers, especially if the agreement was effectively non-binding, as was the case with provisions of the Helsinki Final Act.

Complicating the comparison to OSCE, however, is the fact that, whatever the magnitude of a potential war might have been between the West and the Soviet empire at the time, Europe itself was in a relatively stable situation, divided between two great military blocs. The Helsinki accords were largely meant to codify that situation, not establish a problem-solving institution.[15]

What this means in practice for such a security forum is obvious: on the really tough issues, the forum and guiding principles will matter, but less so than the specific priorities and interests of the states at the time. This dynamic has already showed itself in the Six-Party Talks. Although China clearly had a hand in keeping the talks going, and though the Bush administration's firm intention at the start of the talks was to not be drawn into bilateral discussions with North Korea, it was, in fact, face-to-face talks between the U.S. and North Korea in places like Berlin, Geneva, and New York that produced the 2007 agreement halting North Korea's nuclear program.

This does not mean that such a forum would be without its utility. Nevertheless, there are potential downsides. If, as has been the case with North Korea's nuclear program, the most difficult and important issues are addressed in this ad hoc fashion, the negotiations will undoubtedly involve an ever-shifting alignment of partners as each state enters the discussion with its own set of priorities.[16] This is likely to put more strain on American ties with its treaty partners, not less. Whatever the merits of the accord with North Korea on its nuclear program, it cannot be said that the process of reaching that accord has enhanced U.S. relations with either South Korea or Japan.[17]

Cats and Dogs

China's own views about making the Six-Party Talks more permanent have been mixed: initially, Beijing seemed lukewarm to idea; recently, it has shown more interest. China's willingness to engage in multilateral forums is, of course, a significant change from its Maoist days, when Beijing's diplomacy was far more distrustful of formal entanglements. Nevertheless, it would be an exaggeration to say China's recent change signals a profound transformation of strategic perspective. Beijing picks and chooses its multilateral forums with care. In the case of a new Northeast Asian security forum, for example, China is interested because it would potentially elevate China's regional stature and make the U.S.-Japan alliance less central.[18]

China has also increased ties with ASEAN not only to calm fears about its own growing power in the region—thus heading off a rush into U.S. arms—but also because those ties will give it greater sway in the region over the long run. Initially interested in the idea of the East Asia Summit (the pan-Asian forum held annually since 2005 by the leaders of sixteen countries), Beijing became far less so when Japan, Indonesia, and Singapore insisted that the democracies of India, Australia, and New Zealand be invited as well.[19] Instead, China's diplomats give far more attention to those forums where the PRC's own relative weight is significant and the U.S. role is less prominent or non-existent, as is true of ASEAN Plus Three and the Shanghai Cooperation Organization.[20] Daniel Twining calls the SCO "China's favorite regional forum," while Shulong Chu notes that since APT's start, China has been "more active in APT than it is in the other multilateral organizations in Asia, and it is more active than the other members of the group." In the words of the Chinese foreign ministry, the APT should be "the main channel" for "building an Asian community."[21]

All of which suggests that Chinese multilateralism is highly instrumental. As one scholar has noted: "In the economic realm, [Chinese] multilateralism is secondary to the principle of development for developing countries, including China. In the security arena, multilateralism is subordinate to great power relations." And, "most importantly, in both [areas] multilateralism is subordinate to the principle of state sovereignty."[22] In short, Chinese multilateralism is not driven by some new commitment to liberal internationalism, but by old-fashioned realpolitik and China's desire to stem interference in its own domestic rule. This is not to say that Beijing cannot be convinced to be more cooperative and that institutions might help in that regard, but it does suggest that cooperation with China will be on terms that are more narrowly conceived than many are hoping.

Nor is this to suggest that Washington's own policy in the region has been of a deep commitment to liberal internationalism. As mentioned above, for the most part the U.S. has stuck with a security architecture that revolves around its treaty-defined, hard security commitments to Japan, South Korea, and Australia, as well as less-defined commitments to the Philippines, Thailand, Singapore, and Taiwan.[23] The U.S. has also boosted its ties to Indonesia, Vietnam, Pakistan, and India in recent years. A bilateral and unilateral approach to the region, of course, provides Washington "with greater autonomy than a multilateral approach" and reflects the long-standing view that the region's history and diversity precludes any serious attempts at effective multilateralism.[24] Which is to say: Asia is no Europe.

As a result, recent administrations, including both the Clinton and Bush White Houses, have largely stood on the sidelines when it comes to the region's own efforts to establish multilateral bodies. They have neither fought the trend nor made much of an effort to support it. Indeed, the one forum the U.S. has shown serious interest in, the Asia-Pacific Economic Cooperation forum, reveals the limit of that interest: APEC's focus is almost exclusively economic and its members range far outside Asia to include the likes of Canada, Peru, Chile, and Mexico.[25]

As for the region's other major powers—Japan, Australia, South Korea, and India—their relationships with the U.S. are more uncertain than perhaps at anytime in recent memory. Canberra and Tokyo, for example, see their security as grounded first and foremost in their respective treaty ties to the United States. But they are also working through a vastly more complex relationship with China and neighboring countries. In the case of South Korea, of course, there is even more ambiguity about its future security vision: ties with China have grown significantly, but so have creeping concerns about China's potential dominance. Similarly, reconciliation with North Korea is a top priority for Seoul, but doubts remain about the extent to which that can be accomplished given the nature of the Pyongyang regime. Finally, an increased sense of Korean nationalism is an uneasy fit with a Japan that wants to become a "normal" player on the world stage. Although each of these issues has produced tensions with Washington in recent years, Seoul appears to have increasingly come to see that solid ties with the U.S. are ultimately required if these complex issues are to be addressed satisfactorily.

Finally, there is India—a rising power of its own that believes it is already in a strategic competition with China and hence is looking to expand multilateral and bilateral ties in the region, albeit reluctantly, given its own history of diplomatic self-reliance. In turn, both the Clinton and Bush administrations have seen India as a potential new partner in their hedging strategy vis à vis China. But as C. Raja Mohan succinctly points out: "India's recent attitudes toward the United States have swung between expectations of a natural alliance between two democracies to fears of subordination in a potential partnership with the world's sole superpower."[26]

Given the diversity of strategic approaches to alliances and multilateralism by the two major powers in the region (China and the United States); given the uncertainties of some of the other major powers (Japan, South Korea, and India) about exactly what roles they will play regionally; and, finally, given the diversity of regime types among the remaining powers, it is no surprise that the region has been described as having a "fractured security structure"[27] and that the proliferation of various forums and treaty alignments looks more like a list of cats and dogs than a coherent and predictable framework for the future.

What's Next?

For all the confusion when it comes to understanding the current state of multilateral and bilateral relations within the Asia-Pacific theater, there are three undeniable trends that must be addressed if any new architecture for the region is to have a chance of succeeding. The first is Asia's own desire to create an Asian community of some sort. The past decade has seen various fits and starts on this matter, reflecting both the difficulties of creating such a community and the ever-present pressure to move forward given the growing interdependence and interlocking policy agendas among the states in the areas of economics, security, health, terrorism, and the environment. The second trend is the continuing growth of Chinese power, which demands a policy of both engagement and hedging on the part of its neighbors and, principally, by the United States, since it is the only country powerful enough to do so effectively. Finally, the spread of democracy in the region has inevitably sparked U.S. interest in seeing the democratic Asia-Pacific states become their own "community" as well. Although for both the Clinton and Bush administrations this idea appeared at times to be more a matter of presidential rhetoric than institution-building, it shows no sign of receding from discussions about what should inform the organizational shape of the region in the future.

Squaring each of these trends with the others seems almost impossible. Complicating matters further, as Ralph Cossa points out, are debates over such issues as "Asia-Pacific vs. East Asian regionalism." Should Asia's community consist of Asian countries alone, or should it include the likes of Australia, a Pacific country with vital interests and ties to Asia? How does Washington's traditional alliance-orientated strategy in Asia and its fondness for ad hoc multilateralism (as in the case of the Proliferation Security Initiative) fit with the region's increasing movement toward multilateralism? And finally, what, precisely, is the character of that multilateralism? Again, as Cossa notes, one would be hard pressed to define the "nature of the organizing principles and objectives behind" forums like the East Asia Summit or the ASEAN Plus Three.[28] Given these issues and the cross-trends noted above, it is hardly a surprise that the last two administrations have largely taken a "wait and see" approach to multilateral developments in the Asia-Pacific region.

There is, of course, the possibility that things will naturally fall into place to the U.S.'s advantage in the region. In other words, a rising, autocratic China may inevitably lead the region's democracies (and any number of its smaller states) to turn to the U.S. without much effort on Washington's part.

But there are problems with this bet and opportunity costs if Washington decides to wait for things to fall in place. First, unlike the Soviet Union, China is unlikely to present itself as the kind of overwhelming threat that moves nations to overtly jump on the U.S. bandwagon. To the contrary, both the United States and countries in the region will be heavily engaged with China in the decades ahead, especially economically. The result will be a more complex set of relations that will likely lead more to policy drift than to states making hard strategic choices. Second, China's power in the region will undoubtedly increase relative to that of the United States. As it does, the U.S. ought to be looking for ways to maximize its influence through region-wide forums and institutional arrangements. Well-crafted multilateral organizations can be force multipliers and can help allied states think more seriously about broader common security needs than bilateral relationships typically can. Finally, there are costs to not taking full advantage of the opportunities that the positive trends—such as the spread of liberal economics and politics—in the region present. But doing so requires creating organizations that shape and lock in that change. The most dramatic example of such an effort has been the creation of a Europe "whole and free" through the expansion of both the North Atlantic Treaty Organization (NATO) and the European Union (EU) into Central and Eastern Europe after the collapse of the Soviet Union.

But creating a NATO or EU-like structure for Asia-Pacific is perhaps a bridge too far. As many have pointed out, the differences—historically, culturally, and geopolitically—among the states of the region are probably too significant to accomplish such a feat. Indeed, perhaps the strongest comment to this effect was then-Deputy Secretary of Defense Paul Wolfowitz's statement to journalists in May 2002 that he "certainly" didn't "envision a NATO-like security structure in East Asia. NATO... started, obviously, from a Cold War period when we were allied together against a common enemy. . . . East Asia is a very, very different situation where the diversity of countries, the diversity of interests doesn't call for that kind of structure."[29]

But accepting the fact that the differences between the situation in Asia and Europe are great does not mean that there are not parallel lessons to be drawn. Nor should we assume that, over time, institutions cannot lessen existing differences and modify state behavior. To hear Asia specialists tell it, Japan's "history" problem makes it virtually impossible for it to be accepted by other states in the region as a "normal" country, let alone a leader reflecting its relative level of power. But Japan's history problem is not unlike Germany's following World War II; and today, former Allied and Axis countries— countries that killed millions of each others' citizens—are subjects of one union, whose borders and economies are wide open to each other. Again, it would be wrong to draw strict parallels between Europe and Asia. However, it would be equally incorrect to adopt a form of geo-cultural determinism that ignores the art of the possible when it comes to Asia and the Pacific.

So, the question is: what is possible?

Tier One: a CSCE for Asia
Perhaps the first step in thinking through a multilateral structure for Asia is to recognize that the diversity of regimes in the region means that there will be real limits to what a multilateral organization or forum can accomplish. But that was equally true when the high representatives of thirty-three European countries, the United States, and Canada signed the Final Act of the Conference on Security and Cooperation in Europe (CSCE) in Helsinki on August 1, 1975. While the Cold War was perhaps a little less frigid at the time of the accords' signing, the line between East and West in Europe

was still one of concrete and barbed wire, with millions of men under arms in two opposing blocs—NATO and the Warsaw Pact.

The Helsinki Accords, as they came to be called, were divided into three "baskets." The first dealt with questions related to European security and comprised a declaration of principles designed to guide relations among the signatories. Key among these principles were the abstention from the threat or use of force, the territorial integrity of states, a proposal for a system for dispute resolution, and a modest set of confidence-building measures entailing notification of military maneuvers and the voluntary exchange of observers at military exercises. Basket II concerned cooperation in the field of economics, science, and the environment, while Basket III, among other things, required states to act in conformity with the Universal Declaration of Human Rights and to respect "the inherent dignity of the human person" and the right of individuals "to know and act" on these rights, including the freedom to emigrate from any country. Artfully written and not legally binding, the Final Act did, nevertheless, help create an overall framework for a more stable Europe.[30]

Can a similar accord be crafted for Asia? In fact, Asia is, in some respects, more than halfway there already. On February 24, 1976, the heads of five Southeast Asian states (Indonesia, Singapore, Malaysia, Thailand, and the Philippines) signed the Treaty of Amity and Cooperation (TAC). The guiding principles of the treaty were: "Mutual respect for the independence, sovereignty, equality, territorial integrity and national identity of all nations; the right of every State to lead its national existence free from external interference, subversion or coercion; non-interference in the internal affairs of one another; settlement of differences or disputes by peaceful means; the renunciation of the threat or use of force; and effective cooperation among themselves." Since 1976, all the member states of ASEAN as well as China, India, Japan, Pakistan, Russia, South Korea, and Australia have signed the accord. And, as noted previously, ASEAN, at its summit in November 2007, took the next step in institutionalizing the principles of the TAC by adopting a formal charter for the organization that establishes an ASEAN secretariat headed by a secretary general as well as standing committees in the areas of economics, socio-cultural affairs, and political security. And while the charter renews the original ASEAN commitment to non-interference in the internal affairs of member states and the renunciation of aggression or the threat of force, it also includes commitments on the part of member states to "market economies," "economic integration," "good governance, the principles of democracy and constitutional government," "respect for fundamental freedoms," and "the promotion and protection of human rights."[31]

Of course, because ASEAN's process of decision-making by consensus did not change, some viewed the charter as having failed to lay the ground for a more dynamic and liberal Asian community. But this may well be the charter's virtue. Scaled up and modified as needed, the charter could serve as the defining element for the larger Asian community, whether that community is defined as participants in ASEAN Plus Three or the East Asia Summit. More modest in what it could do or enforce, such a charter would be more acceptable to the diversity of regimes in Asia and the Asia-Pacific region. And, indeed, if the rest of Asia were to signal a willingness to establish an organization along the lines outlined above, China would be hard-pressed not to join, especially given the fact that the U.S. would not be a member.

Although more modest in vision, an Asian charter and organization would still, to a large degree, fulfill Asia's continuing desire to become a "community" of some kind.[32] Moreover, there are plenty of matters that Asia's nations can and should deliberate in common. Disaster relief, the environment, trade, maritime safety, and territorial disputes are just a few of the issues that such an organization could usefully address. The bottom line is that globalization and transnational problems have put a premium on multilateral cooperation. And while such a multilateral forum would be limited in its capacity to tackle more divisive issues, such as the status of Taiwan, it could provide a normative baseline for state behavior that would bring increased stability to the region.

Tier Two: Asia-Pacific Forum of Democracies

A CSCE for Asia has its advantages; but, in the end, it will be of limited utility when it comes to shaping and directing the region's future. Engaging in dialogue and setting norms are important, but neither can hope to deepen or expand the gains made by democrats in the region. Nor, frankly, can America's bilateral security ties with Japan, South Korea, or Australia. These are, as Bisley notes, "fairly blunt" security instruments and are a poor bridge to the range of policy matters of concern to the democracies in the region.[33] And while a NATO for Asia might be out of the question at the moment, a new multilateral "club" of Asian-Pacific democracies ought not to be.

In some respects, the region is already primed for such an organization. Public opinion polls taken across the region by the East Asia Barometer, for example, indicate that democracy is the preferred form of government by a majority of populations residing outside of China.[34] In addition, a slow but maturing series of ministerial meetings has taken place between Japan, Australia, and the United States since 2006. Japan also inked a strategic accord with India in 2006 and signed a formal security pact with Australia in 2007. And, more recently, Washington and Tokyo have asked Australia to consider expanding the trilateral sessions into a quadrilateral dialogue including India.[35]

But to truly construct what the Bush administration has called "a balance of power that favors freedom" in Asia will require more than ministerial meetings and bilateral accords.[36] As others have noted, "there is a perception in Asia that America's laser-like focus on defeating terrorism causes it to talk past allies primarily concerned with fueling Asia's economic dynamism." In contrast, Beijing has talked economics first and "its influence has increased accordingly."[37] A good place to start, then, is the creation of a free-trade area between the United States, Japan, and the other democratic states of the Asia-Pacific region. Membership in the arrangement would be governed by adherence to a set of liberal criteria in governance as well as trade.[38] As with the European Union, the lure of access to markets should provide an incentive structure for states to become (and stay) members in good standing. In addition, the organization could establish tools, as in the OSCE, to monitor elections, provide peacekeeping forces, coordinate humanitarian operations and non-proliferation efforts, and generally provide a forum for enhanced but still voluntary security cooperation among the democracies. As such, it would not attempt to replace existing bilateral security treaty arrangements, but would serve as a substantial "soft power" overlay tying the countries together.

Taking a two-tiered multilateral approach in Asia means that the states in the region are not forced to choose between China and the United States. Countries can have a foot in both forums, creating a multilateral architecture that reflects the need to both engage China and hedge against its rise.

There are further advantages to such an approach. First, it provides a forum for Japan to ease into becoming a "normal" country—fitting its desire to play a larger role on the world stage but in a way that reassures other states of its limited and pacific intentions. Second, it provides India a mechanism for maintaining its formal "in-dependent" foreign and defense policies—a point of pride for the rising power—but in a way that allows it to work more closely with the United States, as it sees fit. Instead of force-feeding the relation-ship with grand bilateral programs and initiatives, it allows New Delhi and Washington to build from the bottom up. Third, a re-gional democratic forum could bridge the gap between Seoul's un-derstanding of its security in terms largely confined to the penin-sula and Washington's view of the issue through a broader strategic lens, helping to reintegrate South Korea into its more natural asso-ciation with the other democratic powers in the region. Fourth, a club of democracies could finally help prevent Taiwan's slide into deeper and deeper international isolation by providing a place for it to interact and cooperate with the other democracies in the region. Making Taipei more confident about its place in the world is a neces-sary step in preventing it from taking sudden initiatives to reassert itself in the face of what it sees as affronts to its existing sovereignty. Finally, establishing a multilateral organization with liberal political criteria for maintaining membership and structured incentives for doing so can be important in consolidating democratic gains in countries like Indonesia and potentially preventing the kind of back-sliding one sees in states such as the Philippines or Thailand.

China will complain that such an arrangement is a form of con-tainment. To meet that complaint, or at least mitigate it somewhat, Washington should define this new effort as providing public goods to the region that would otherwise either be provided serendipitously or not at all—a point that has the benefit of actually being true.

That said, Beijing already reads Washington's policy of strength-ening ties with allies in the region, building new relations with Viet-nam and India, and pressing NATO into Central Asia as a form of encirclement. And, to the extent that China's military and economic power continues to grow, future American administrations will in-creasingly be forced to take concrete steps to reassure allies and friends of its presence in the region. Indeed, all of this is virtually inevitable. It would be more prudent to design a multilateral archi-tecture that takes advantage of the democratic strengths we have in hand now than to play the great power game in an ad hoc and reac-tive fashion. If, over the coming decades, China doesn't liberalize, Washington will have set in place a framework that will allow it to speed security cooperation in the region as it becomes necessary. If China does, there will be a ready-made structure for it to integrate itself into the existing liberal international order.

Conclusion

The problem with Washington's current approach to Asia-Pacific multilateralism is that it has neither kept up with China's increased levels of engagement throughout the region nor sufficiently kept ahead of that country's growing hard power. The U.S. often appears to be a day late and a dollar short when it comes to seeing and then reacting to trends and events in the region. That, in truth, cannot be said about U.S. policy toward India, which under both the Clin-ton and Bush administrations has been quite forward leaning. Here the issue is whether the actual policy approach is one best suited to building a long-term relationship that fits both India's need to see itself as a recognized great power and, yet, increasingly integrates it into a global liberal order that supports the shared security interests of New Delhi, Washington, and its other allies. And, finally, Washington has talked a good game over the years about the revolution in democratic governance in Asia but has done too little to reinforce it and take advantage of it. If American policymakers believe, as they say they do, in the theory of the "democratic peace," then it is strategically shortsighted to continue to treat the Asia-Pacific region as though it was closer to Mars than just on the other side of the globe from Europe.[39]

The two-tiered approach to the Asia-Pacific region spelled out above will provide a more adequate framework for U.S. policy down the road, recognizing as it does the complexity of U.S. and neighboring states' relations with China, while at the same time reassuring the region of our commitment to stay engaged on the basis of principles that serve our long-term interests.

CHAPTER SIX

THE RISE OF TAIWAN

What's Left of the "One China" Policy?

Ellen Bork

I n the eyes of U.S. officials, the chief virtue of America's Taiwan policy is its immutability. "U.S. policy on Taiwan remains constant, and that is that we have a 'one China' policy, based on three communiqués," Secretary of State Condoleezza Rice said in Beijing in November 2005, more than 30 years after the first of these, the 1972 Shanghai Communiqué, was agreed to by Richard Nixon and Mao Zedong.[1]

Although "hardly anyone ever reads the texts of these documents anymore,"[2] the documents on which the "one China" policy is based, and to which Secretary Rice referred—the Shanghai Communiqué of 1972 and the subsequent 1979 and 1982 communiqués—have acquired the status of "sacred texts."[3] Even the Taiwan Relations Act, passed by Congress to provide a framework for unofficial relations with Taiwan after President Jimmy Carter's formal break in relations with the island in 1979, has never been amended, despite Taiwan's democratization and the immense changes in the strategic balance of power in the Taiwan Strait.

For more than thirty years, Washington has clung to a policy adopted to meet the perceived strategic needs of 1972. These unrevised texts defy efforts to adapt policy to fit new circumstances. The rigid adherence to the language of "one China" has stunted discourse on China and Taiwan policy. Deviations from the rote language of the policy typically elicit dismissal from the small group of policy experts and officials who reserve to themselves the right of interpretation. "The language on Taiwan is very arcane, very nuanced, and people are apt to make mistakes with it," Winston Lord, a former American ambassador to China, said in a condescending rebuff to President George W. Bush's 2001 statement that he would do "whatever it took" to defend Taiwan.[4] However, if on that occasion the president strayed outside the blurry lines of America's "strategic ambiguity," not a few other senior officials have also misstated the official position, though usually at Taiwan's expense.

American officials have pursued the "one China" policy even as developments in China and Taiwan have made it an unworkable, even dangerous, anachronism. What changed to make the policy so inapplicable? And why is a policy intended to maintain "the status quo" so destabilizing instead? To begin such an inquiry, a review of the "one China" language from the 1972 Shanghai Communiqué is helpful:

> The United States acknowledges that all Chinese on either side of the Taiwan Strait maintain there is but one China and that Taiwan is part of China. The United States Government does not challenge that position. It reaffirms its interest in a peaceful settlement of the Taiwan question by the Chinese themselves.[5]

U.S. acquiescence to Beijing's position was not based on substantive agreement about Taiwan, but on strategic calculations. The U.S. wanted to win the cooperation of the People's Republic of China (PRC) on Vietnam and to prevent a rapprochement between the PRC and the Soviet Union, keeping China on the U.S. side, or at least out of the Cold War.

Many accounts show just how far the U.S. was prepared to go to garner China's cooperation. On his first, secret visit to Beijing in 1971, then-National Security Advisor Henry Kissinger agreed that Taiwan was part of China, and asserted that the U.S. did not support "two Chinas" or a "one China, one Taiwan" solution.[6] During his 1972 visit, Nixon himself privately promised Chairman Mao that he would normalize relations with Beijing in his second term and withdraw all American forces from Taiwan; but he also stressed that he could not make that public in the communiqué. "I must be able to go back to Washington," he told Zhou Enlai, "and say that no secret deals have been made."[7] Further assurances were given in private to Beijing, including Washington's intention to terminate eventually the U.S.-Republic of China defense treaty.

The brief passage from the Shanghai Communiqué quoted above has both guided and constrained U.S. policy for more than three decades, despite enormous changes in the geopolitical situation. The language of "one China" has had far-reaching implications, creating, as Richard C. Bush has written, a "substantive asymmetry" with Washington, in effect conceding the matter as a domestic Chinese affair, rather than one of international concern.[8]

Furthermore, as Bush writes, the language of "one China" set in motion a dynamic that has characterized U.S.-China policy ever since—an uneasy, ultimately untenable dynamic in which Beijing acts as "*demandeur* and the United States . . . [is] on the defensive."[9] From Beijing's point of view, with Washington having acknowledged the PRC's position in public—not to mention agreeing to it in private—the U.S. should publicly accept Beijing's sovereignty over Taiwan. Subsequent policies—the 1979 recognition of the PRC, the break in relations with the Republic of China (ROC), President Ronald Reagan's 1982 pledge to phase out arms sales, and President Bill Clinton's "three no's"[10]—have all flowed from the original "one China" accommodation, and were all a product of this dynamic in which China demands, and the U.S. gradually yields ground.

Yet arguably the most serious, if underappreciated, aspect of the "one China" agreement is its treatment of the people of Taiwan. Washington's "acknowledgement" of "one China" created the presumption in U.S. policy that people on both sides of the strait considered themselves "Chinese" and were committed to the unification of China and Taiwan. But this was not the case, as many American regional experts knew quite well. As the draft text of the Shanghai Communiqué was circulated internally, "irate" American diplomats "pointed out that many native Taiwanese did not agree with the Nationalist government's position that Taiwan was part of China," writes James Mann. Unaware of the private assurances given by Nixon and Kissinger, they suggested rewording the document to—at the very least—make a distinction between the people of Taiwan and the people of China. Their views were rebuffed by the PRC and Washington acquiesced. "Thus," writes Mann, "the communiqué did not so much as hint at the existence of the Taiwanese who make up four-fifths of the population of the island."[11] Of all the problems created by an unrevised, outdated Taiwan policy, the failure to recognize the existence, not to mention the wishes, of the majority of the Taiwanese population is the most urgent.

The Development of a Taiwanese Identity

Understanding Taiwanese identity is no easy task.[12] Its origins and definition seem as varied as the academic disciplines brought to bear to study it. Generally, national identity is viewed as the product of Taiwan's own history and experiences, which, during the long separation from China, led to a culture somewhat distinct from Han culture and, in turn, an identity that was not simply Chinese. This difference in identity was reinforced by the conflict between the native Taiwanese and the authoritarian, discriminatory rule of the mainlanders under the Kuomintang (KMT) following World War II.[13] Some trace the beginnings of a Taiwanese identity back to Japanese colonial rule of the island, while others note the effect of the Korean War on Taiwan, during which the U.S. first placed a protective cordon around the island.[14] And, finally, others argue that Taiwanese identity is shaped not only by the islanders' experiences but by

> what they missed: the key events that shaped the national consciousness of the Chinese, including the collapse of the Qing, Sun Yat-sen's revolutionary efforts, warlord depredations, the literary revolution of the May 4th Movement, the glory of the Northern Expedition, and the myth of national unity during the War of Resistance.[15]

Daniel C. Lynch has noted the importance to Taiwanese scholars of Benedict Anderson's concept of "imagined community."[16] In this case, there is less emphasis on the traditional attributes of nationhood and more on a "constructed" model. The notion of an "imagined" nation—in this case, the "idea" of Taiwan—is attractive to a people who must constantly deal with the implications of their country's being denied diplomatic relations with most of the world and the irredentist claims of a far larger neighbor. All of these approaches seek in one fashion or another to explain the impact that the formative events of Taiwan's recent history—Japanese rule, the nationalist dictatorship, and democratization—have had on Taiwanese identity and, conversely, the Taiwanese's own understanding of their relationship to the mainland.

As a matter of history, Taiwan has not been governed from a mainland capital since the end of the 19th century, when Japan took control of Taiwan as part of the 1895 settlement of the Sino-Japanese war. Prior to that, the reach of Chinese imperial rule was weak. The large majority of Taiwan's people, approximately 85 percent, are descended from 17th- and 18th-century immigrants from the Chinese coastal provinces of Fujian and Guangdong. Only 15 percent are known as "mainlanders," that is, those who arrived with the fleeing KMT after 1949 or their descendants.

While brutal and repressive, Japanese colonial rule marked Taiwan in important ways. Japanese rule is credited with giving Taiwan comparatively advanced systems of education, law, agriculture, and banking. It also left Taiwan with an urban middle class, as well as a standard of living significantly higher than that enjoyed on the mainland. Japanese rule was also the first experience that the Taiwanese had with effective, centralized rule of the island; yet, at the same time, it set in place the rudiments of self-government at the local level.[17] For that reason, Japanese rule simultaneously enhanced the sense that the island's residents had had of separation from the mainland culturally, politically, and economically—while, because of the occupation, also planting the seeds of Taiwanese nationalism.[18]

Following World War II and the defeat of Japan, the KMT-led Republic of China then the recognized government on the mainland —was given "administrative" control of the island by the United Nations Relief and Rehabilitation Authority. Many of the island's urban residents resented the often poor, rural, and illiterate KMT conscripts who arrived from the mainland as part of the effort to assert the ROC's control.[19] At the same time, the ROC-KMT leadership regarded the local Taiwanese with condescension, suspicion, and resentment. The fact that there were some Taiwanese who, as members of the Japanese military, had participated in Japan's atrocities against the Chinese during the war no doubt contributed to sour relations between the islanders and those who had just come from the mainland. Under a governor appointed by Chiang Kai-shek, the people of Taiwan were subjected to a number of harsh measures, including widespread property confiscations and rampant KMT "carpetbagging." With resentment building among the island's population, an uprising was sparked by KMT agents harassing a street vendor. The violent crackdown that took place on February 28, 1947 (which resulted in thousands of deaths), profoundly alienated the Taiwanese and, in turn, increased the island population's own sense of a separate identity.

The repression that subsequently took place (and which began even before Chiang and his KMT forces were forced to flee the mainland in 1949 as Mao's Chinese Communist Party took control) was justified by the KMT as a necessary step in ensuring that the island and the mainland were truly and irretrievably unified. Not surprisingly, KMT policies had a distinctly cultural aspect. Indeed, Chiang and the KMT elite considered the people of Taiwan in dire need of Chinese cultural revival. As a result, they began a program of "Sinification," denigrating the island's local customs and language. Not only was Mandarin, which most Taiwanese did not speak, imposed as the official language, but their own language was treated as inferior and vulgar.[20] Streets were renamed with place-names from the mainland, reflecting both the KMT's contempt for the Taiwanese and Chiang's increasingly deluded vision of regaining control of the Chinese mainland.[21] Naturally, these policies only increased the islanders' sense of isolation.[22]

If language, culture, and history were the first points of engagement in the battle against oppressors, it is hard to escape the conclusion that a distinct Taiwanese identity was "essentially a political phenomenon."[23] During its dictatorship, the KMT had "the incontestable . . . power to define Taiwan's 'identity' to the island's inhabitants and to the outside world."[24] The identity the KMT defined for Taiwan was nationalist Chinese, rooted in the KMT's chauvinism and ambition to join Taiwan and the mainland under the rule of the Republic of China.

Although Japanese colonization and KMT dictatorship helped form a Taiwanese national identity, the process of democratization on the island arguably transformed it. As Taiwan shed its dictatorship, the culture and history of the majority began to assert itself. Efforts to address—and diminish—the dominance of the mainlanders' culture accompanied the transition. There began to be an "increased emphasis of Taiwanese, rather than Chinese, history and geography in textbooks, the increased used of the Minnan language rather than Mandarin in daily discourse and political campaigning and other moves aimed at desinification."[25]Academic work that was prohibited under the KMT's dictatorship flourished. Taiwanese intellectuals began to address what they felt were distortions of the island's history.

Compensating for what they believed was the "intentional peripher-alization" of Taiwan, they sought to correct the histories that mini-mized the island's importance and its subordination to China.[26]

The affirmation of a Taiwanese identity naturally affected party politics. Even before martial law was lifted in 1987, Chiang Ching-kuo, Chiang Kai-shek's son and successor, recognized the ultimately unsustainable position of the KMT as a minority, mainlander-based ruling party. He appointed native Taiwanese to party and govern-ment positions and later permitted opposition activity. Today, the KMT's ranks are mostly composed of native Taiwanese. And KMT politicians who were born on the mainland, or whose parents were, face the electoral necessity of appealing to the majority of native Taiwanese.

However, it was Chiang Ching-kuo's chosen successor, Lee Teng-hui who is most responsible for introducing the idea of Taiwanese national identity into the political arena. Despite being a native Tai-wanese himself, Lee did not resort to a narrow, ethnically exclusive vision of Taiwanese identity. Instead, he articulated an inclusive identity, accommodating both the Taiwanese historical experience and its contemporary democratic achievement. "I now refer to my fellow citizens as 'New Taiwanese,'" he wrote, "meaning those who are willing to fight for the prosperity and survival of their country, regardless of when they or their forebears arrived on Taiwan and re-gardless of their provincial heritage or native language."[27]

Lee's concept of "new Taiwanese" resonated enough with the is-landers that the heir to the KMT leadership, Ma Ying-jeou, adopted it during his successful 1998 campaign for mayor of Taipei. In an act of high political theater during a campaign rally, Lee asked Ma, in Mandarin Chinese, whether he was a mainlander or a Taiwanese. Ma, the son of mainlander parents, famously responded in the Tai-wanese language that he was a "new Taiwanese."[28]

While it is the Democratic Progressive Party (DPP) that is re-garded as exploiting Taiwanese identity for political purposes, in fact, both political camps now agree that both ethnic Taiwanese and mainlanders living on the island share a common Taiwanese identity.[29] "These politicians did not invent this identity," writes scholar Melissa J. Brown, "They merely articulated and emphasized a change in Taiwanese identity that had been developing" during the period of democratization.[30] Indeed, according to a public opinion poll taken by the National Chengchi University in 2004, 41.5 percent of respondents identified themselves as Taiwanese, up from just 17.3 percent in 1993. In this same period, the share of those who called themselves Chinese fell by more than half, to less than 10 percent.[31]

These developments are significant, even if all of their causes and implications are not clear. Admittedly, it can be difficult to know precisely what significance an individual may attach to the labels "Taiwanese" or "Chinese." Moreover, the two are not mutually exclusive. A consistently large number of people, in fact, identify themselves as both.[32] But research also shows the different significance, or association, that the people of Taiwan attach to their Taiwanese and Chinese identities.

> "China" and "Taiwan" both remain part of the people's subjective understanding of what their national identity is, although they apparently attach different dimensions of national identity to each. Whereas "China" is often identified with the ethnocultural underpinnings of the Taiwanese nation, "Taiwan" is foremost understood in historical and political terms.[33]

Increasingly, Taiwanese identity is bound up in the people's commitment to, or identification with, the democratic state.

The implications for the island's political parties are unavoidable: Platforms and rhetoric may vary, but neither major party in Taiwan can diverge from the position that Taiwan is a de facto independent, sovereign, democratic state. Likewise, no major political party on Taiwan can afford to be seen accepting a version of the "one China" policy that fundamentally compromises Taiwanese self-rule. Hence, while the KMT platform still calls for unification of the island with the mainland, the party's head has conditioned that unification on China becoming a democracy and only if consented to by the people of Taiwan.[34] The decision by the Chen administration to hold a referendum on seeking membership in the United Nations under the name Taiwan is another example of this trend. Despite the opposition of Washington and Beijing to the referendum, which many see as a prelude to a referendum on independence, the KMT's reaction was not to be seen as any less concerned with asserting the country's sovereignty. It devised its own referendum proposal calling for UN membership under the name of the Republic of China.[35] Party leaders could argue about which of the two parties was more likely to have success in dealing with Washington and Beijing, but neither party was willing to be seen as doing so at the price of Taiwan's sovereignty. "Consequently," as a matter of Taiwanese policy toward China, "it does not make much difference which party governs the island, when the political future of Taiwan is the issue."[36]

Taiwanese Identity and the "One China" Policy

Washington has not adjusted to the consensus Taiwan's people have forged regarding Taiwan's sovereignty and the island's future. Abroad, the development of a Taiwanese identity is often seen as the product of narrow party politics, pro-independence activism, or as a phenomenon confined to ethnic Taiwanese. The assertion of a Taiwanese identity draws skepticism and even alarm within American foreign policy and academic circles long accustomed to viewing Taiwan through the "one China" lens. As with most things Taiwanese, they are perceived first and foremost with regard to how they affect tensions between Taiwan and China or relations between the U.S. and China.

Taiwan's "self-conscious nation-building project," is often considered intellectually suspect and even reckless. One scholar has even called it "suicidally quixotic" with the "potential to become a great tragedy."[37] Efforts to express a Taiwanese identity are seen as gratuitous, adding "very little value" to Taiwan's free society and prosperity, and more often than not ascribed to the partisan machinations of the Democratic Progressive Party. In this view, China's belligerence is of concern mainly insofar as it is capitalized on by Taiwanese politicians.[38]

It isn't entirely surprising that the rise of a Taiwanese identity causes discomfort in Washington. There is considerable apprehension that the push by the DDP and others to reinforce the notion of a Taiwanese identity is part of a not-so-hidden agenda whose ultimate goal is Taiwanese formal independence. Should that be the result, there is ample reason to fear that China would react with force, potentially involving the U.S. in a conflict to defend Taiwan. Or, even if a formal declaration of independence were not the result, there is no question that Taiwan's development of a self-confident, self-sufficient national personality might still provoke Beijing into taking military action as it sees the island slipping further and further from its grasp.

These fears, however, are in large part the predictable by-product of Washington's "one China" policy. Viewing Taiwanese identity through the prism of the "one China" policy distorts reality. As Shelley Rigger has written, discussions of Taiwanese identity often "conflate and confuse" different elements of Taiwanese identity, leading to misconceptions about the issue of greatest concern to U.S. policymakers:

> Many observers suspect that the growing tendency for Taiwan residents to call themselves Taiwanese, as opposed to Chinese or both, reveals a widening rift between the people of Taiwan and the idea of a unified China. Another widespread suspicion is that the promotion of Taiwan nationality is part of a strategy aimed at achieving formal independence for the island.[39]

According to Rigger, assumptions about the implications of particular aspects of identity—that is, for example, whether one considers oneself Taiwanese or Chinese—do not correspond to attitudes about independence. Rigger argues that "[A]t least some of the data on nationality suggests that equating 'Taiwanese' identity with support for independence is a mistake. To begin with, statistics purporting to show how Taiwanese identify themselves cannot capture the

full spectrum of meanings respondents associate with these catego-
ries."[40] In fact, Taiwanese identity appears to be quite pragmatic and
is conditioned by such other considerations as the citizens' sense of
security, the state of the economy, and political developments.[41]

Unfortunately, this explication of Taiwanese identity can only go
so far toward calming nerves in Washington. As Rigger notes, the
Taiwanese "commitment to democracy is stronger than their determination to achieve a particular outcome."[42] Taiwanese identity is
tightly linked to the island's democracy, or to a *"political* community."[43] The nature of Taiwanese identity, in other words, is "liberal
and civic."[44] But, as such, it is virtually impossible to imagine a for-
mula for unification that would satisfy Beijing's aspiration to exercise sovereignty over the island without coming into conflict with
the Taiwanese desire to be a self-governing people. And as long as
Taiwan is self-governing, its population will inevitably think of itself
as an independent people—a fact that is a direct challenge to the
"one China" policy as enunciated either in Washington or Beijing.

U.S.-Taiwan Relations in the Past

At this point, it is helpful to point out that despite the evident flaws
in the "one China" policy and Washington's close relationship with
Chiang Kai-shek and the KMT dictatorship, the U.S. has been crucial to Taiwan's democratization. Washington's considerable, if ambiguous, commitment to the island's defense, which began during the Korean War, continues to this day. There is no doubt that,
throughout the period of the KMT dictatorship, Washington saw
U.S.-Taiwan policy as a tradeoff between maintaining security and
encouraging increased respect for human and political rights on the
island, with the former more often than not taking priority over the
latter.[45] Nevertheless, it is also the case that U.S. economic and military aid was used to support Taiwan's long-term process of liberalization and reform.[46]

Indeed, at times, Washington's preference for reformers became
a sore spot in relations with Taipei. Deeply suspicious of American

influence, Chiang considered liberal, Western-leaning members of his government dangerous and vulnerable to American co-option. When it came to democracy, he had much more in common with Mao than with his American protectors. "Chiang detested liberal democracy for a number of reasons," writes John Garver, "not the least of which was, he believed, that it would interfere with the 'sacred mission' of liberating the mainland from Communist rule."[47]

Nevertheless, Washington promoted economic and political reforms intended to encourage democratic development in Taiwan.[48] Ultimately, it was the Generalissimo's son, Chiang Ching-kuo, who took steps toward democratic reforms, believing them necessary to Taiwan's domestic governance as well as to mitigating Taiwan's isolation as a result of the U.S.-China rapprochement.[49]

It is also worth recalling that before Washington adopted the "one China" policy, there was an extended period during which the U.S. took a much different view. During the years 1950–1972, as Richard C. Bush has written, Washington tried to "gain acceptance of the idea that there were, or might be, more or less equal political entities on each side of the Taiwan Strait," and at least for a time considered the people of Taiwan, the Formosans, as deserving of some form of self-determination.[50]

As Bush has recounted, after World War II, the U.S. and its allies initially decided that Taiwan would be returned to China, which at the time they recognized as Chiang's ROC. However, after war broke out on the Korean peninsula, Washington argued that Taiwan should be a matter resolved by the international community, rather than handled as a purely domestic Chinese concern.[51]

In the summer of 1950, the U.S. proposed a UN commission to address the issue.[52] Secretary of State Dean Acheson argued that the U.S. and other democracies were "entitled to question the turning of Formosa over to such [a] regime [the PRC] without consulting Formosans or applying principles of UN Charter applicable to dependent peoples."[53] Anticipating resistance from Great Britain on the grounds that Taiwan's fate had already been settled, Acheson argued that, among other things, "the People's Republic of China was an animal very different from the Republic of China, which was the Chinese party at the Cairo conference."[54]

The effort to establish the UN commission foundered. However, for a time, the U.S. used the well-being and self-determination of the people of Taiwan to argue a position that is diametrically opposed to the one Washington is so wedded to today. Although, according to Richard Bush, this "was the last time the U.S. definition of Taiwan's status was so focused on the need to give the people of the island a say over their own destiny,"[55] for most of the next two decades, the United States did *not* follow a "one China" policy.

Even later, when Washington was moving toward establishing ties with the PRC, the U.S. tried to deal with the difficult question of UN membership by proposing "dual representation." Then-U.S. ambassador to the UN George H.W. Bush argued, "We face a reality, not a theory" when it comes to cross-strait relations. "Our proper concern must be" to address the fact that there are two "effective governing entities," the PRC and the Republic of China on Taiwan.[56]

Toward a New Taiwan Policy

Washington's goal of maintaining the supposed status quo in the Taiwan Strait is an illusion. From its inception, the "one China" policy was based on an erroneous premise: that Taiwan and its people belonged to China and were willing to come under its rule, be it by the CCP or the KMT. Over the course of a century, the Taiwanese developed a separate identity through historical and political experiences quite different from those on the mainland. Taiwan is now a full-fledged democracy. It has held presidential and national legislative elections for more than a decade and, in the 2000 presidential election, accomplished the first transition of power from the KMT to the former opposition, the DPP. Since 1992, the ROC no longer claims sovereignty over the mainland. Taiwan has discarded not only the KMT dictatorship but also its Chinese chauvinism. And in place of an imposed Chinese national identity, a new identity, rooted in Taiwan's democracy, has arisen on the island.

Furthermore, the strategic circumstances that led the U.S. to adopt the "one China" policy no longer exist. The Cold War rationale for using China as a counterweight against the Soviet Union has obviously disappeared. There is no "China card" for the U.S. to play anymore. China has grown stronger economically, and its ambitions toward Taiwan have taken on greater significance as the CCP seeks legitimacy at home. China's military, long thought to pose no threat to Taiwan, is assiduously acquiring new capabilities designed for just that purpose. Whether China is capable of undertaking an amphibious invasion of Taiwan is open to debate; what is not open to debate, however, is China's growing capacity to conduct various coercive measures designed to bring Taiwan to heel. Politically, the PRC maintains that Taiwan is a part of China. Beijing has stated that the conditions under which it would consider the use of force against Taiwan include not only a declaration of independence by Taiwan but also conditions that fall short of that—such as, if "possibilities for a peaceful reunification should be completely exhausted."[57]

America's "one China" policy is not only at odds with the reality in Taiwan but also with its own larger vision of the democratic peace. The Bush administration, which came into office pledging to place greater importance on reinvigorated alliances with long-time partners, made marginal progress on that front. Even before entering the White House, George W. Bush articulated a new vision for America's relationships in Asia, speaking of a "fellowship of free Pacific nations as strong and united as our European partnership."[58] This unmistakable reference to NATO, coupled with Secretary of State Condoleezza Rice's 2005 call for a new democratic multilateralism, suggested an ambitious change in course from America's traditional bilateral approach to its alliances in Asia.[59] Unlike Europe, Asia has never had a multilateral organization committed to the survival of its democracies.

Although there have been tentative efforts to lay the ground work for such an approach, the idea has not progressed very far. At the end of the second Bush term, the president's democracy agenda encountered serious obstacles: it had been criticized for its contradictions and uneven application; there had been a growing, coordinated backlash from authoritarian regimes against the agenda; and, finally, America's difficulties in Iraq had tainted the world's perception of it.

But there exists no greater obstacle to a coherent democracy agenda than the "one China" policy. Instead of supporting the status quo, the U.S. should state its support not only for Taiwan's democracy but also for the implications of this democracy, namely that Taiwan's people must be able to determine their own future. Despite praising Taiwan's democratic achievement, official U.S. policy does not explicitly support democracy's survival on the island or a democratic determination of Taiwan's future. President Bill Clinton made a welcome attempt at advancing this idea in 2000, when he asserted that "the issues between Beijing and Taiwan must be resolved peacefully and with the assent of the people of Taiwan."[60] This sentiment has been repeated on occasion, but never put on par with official statements such as the three communiqués. Washington has always regarded maintaining peace in the region and supporting democracy on the island as separate, unrelated objectives. Unless and until Washington joins these two together, Beijing will believe that Washington will sacrifice the latter to preserve the former.

Washington must take an aggressive approach to breaking down the taboos and presumptions that the "one China" policy has engrained in the public understanding of Taiwan. The notion of Taiwanese identity as "provocative" must be abandoned and the language that American officials use about Taiwan must change from defensive to unapologetic. Washington must acknowledge Taiwan's identity as a welcome by-product of the island's democratization. Taiwan has never been able to bring itself fully into line with its democratic identity, nor, given the ambiguity of U.S. policy and the resulting precariousness that Taiwan faces internationally, has it been able to engage in the multilateral processes that other emerging democracies have found vital. Washington must include Taiwan in regional diplomacy and organizations commensurate with its democratic status. These could include Taiwan's full participation as a core member of the Proliferation Security Initiative; its inclusion in new democracy-based multilateral organizations; a sincere effort to bring Taiwan into the World Health Organization; and the negotiation of a free-trade agreement. Also, building on the U.S. position advanced by George H.W. Bush in 1971 when he was U.S. ambassador to the UN, the U.S. should revisit the idea of Taiwan's membership in the United Nations. In theory, such membership would not preclude some kind of future accommodation by the island state with the mainland, nor is it inconsistent with how the U.S. and other nations have dealt with other "divided states" in the past. These steps should serve as part of an incremental process of changing Taiwan's international status, making the situation more stable, not less.

Washington must develop a broader and deeper relationship with Taipei so that Taiwan can enjoy a more normal relationship with the United States. Under current policy, U.S. secretaries of defense and state do not visit Taiwan, and the visits of senior Taiwanese officials to the U.S., not to mention those of Taiwan's president, are tightly circumscribed. Changing this will help to raise awareness of Taiwan among the American public, something especially necessary considering the lack of diplomatic relations between Washington and Taipei, and Taiwan's precarious international status. Moreover, more high-level exchanges are in America's interest. Tightly circumscribed communication between the two countries has led, and will continue to lead, to needless misunderstandings—a dangerous problem considering both Taiwan's security importance in the region and the evolving security dilemma in the Taiwan Strait.

The U.S. has not made a sufficient effort to make Taiwan's importance as a free society clear. Nor, for that matter, has Taiwan. Dependent as Taiwan is on American support, its officials are often concerned about overstepping the bounds that are placed on them in operating in the United States. The image of a powerful Taiwan lobby no longer accurately reflects reality and, in any case, has long been out of step with the more important image of Taiwan as a young democracy. Taiwan exists in a kind of purgatory, in which it operates as a full-fledged democracy but is not allowed to take its place among other democratic success stories, like those of Central and Eastern Europe.

In March 2008, the Taiwanese elected Ma Ying-jeou, the KMT candidate and former mayor of Taipei, to succeed Chen Shui-bian as president of the Republic of China. For many in America's governing circles, Ma's election was a relief. Under President Chen, cross-strait relations had grown tense. Both Beijing and Washington saw Chen's efforts to assert a Taiwanese national identity as a not-so-subtle rejection of the "one China" policy. In contrast, as a candidate President Ma pledged to seek better ties with the mainland and the U.S. by not challenging that policy.

Yet, political realities being what they are, Ma also made clear that unification with the mainland was out of the question during his time as president, that he would do nothing to undermine the country's sovereignty, and that, ultimately, it was up to the citizens of the island to decide Taiwan's future. Despite the fact that Ma won the presidential vote by a large margin, he is ultimately limited by the fact that poll after poll indicates that the Taiwanese consider themselves a distinct, self-governing polity and want to keep it that way. To pretend otherwise, as the "one China" policy does, is to create expectations about an eventual solution to cross-strait relations that can't be met. If the "one China" policy was flawed when the U.S. adopted it, it has been rendered untenable by the end of the KMT dictatorship and the assertion of a Taiwanese democratic identity.

CHAPTER SEVEN

WILL CHINA (CONTINUE TO) RISE?

Nicholas Eberstadt

In informed circles the world over, the widely shared presumption is that the People's Republic of China will be a rising power for decades to come. Although particular assessments differ, the expectations are that China's dynamic economic development will continue and that its growing economic potential will be translated into both increasing military might and progressively greater international influence. The economic and strategic rise of China over both the medium- and the long-term is today regarded as the most likely prospect by eminent American and international scholars,[1] by planners and intelligence analysts in the United States government,[2] and—not incidentally—by the Chinese leaders themselves.[3]

The received wisdom about China's ascent may well prove correct. But there are other plausible possibilities as well. A rigorous "contrarian" conspectus of some of the possible "downside" factors that might complicate, hinder, or entirely forestall the rise of Chinese power (economic, political, and/or military) would seem an entirely worthwhile exercise, even if its only purpose were as a discipline in thinking. Such exercises, however, have other virtues: they can lessen the risk of "strategic surprise" precipitated by plausible, but largely unexpected, events.[4] Less than two decades ago, expert opinion in scholarly and policy circles around the world was taken by surprise by the sudden collapse of the Soviet Union. Surely it behooves us today to contemplate alternative futures for the great and rising power that China is so generally taken to be.

This brief chapter will not address the many plausible "alternative futures" to a rising China that might deserve consideration. Instead, we will very briefly note some of the plausible factors that might cloud China's horizons in the decades ahead—without assigning any probability to such adverse developments. We will then shift gears, and move to a much more detailed examination of one particular set of trends bearing on China's future rise: namely, its demographic outlook. This seemingly idiosyncratic focus is justified on at least three grounds. First, unlike almost all other future contingencies for China, the demographic outlook for the country over the next two decades has a high degree of regularity and even predictability. Second, China's demographics have been largely neglected by those who share the vision of a rising China over the coming generation. Third, the implications of China's demographic outlook are on balance clearly unfavorable from the standpoint of the accumulation and projection of state power—perhaps even seriously so.

"Wild Cards" For China's Future Rise

Perhaps the most dramatic future contingency to be considered would be a collapse of the existing Chinese Communist regime. In the abstract, there is nothing absurd about the notion of a wholesale failure of one Chinese governmental directorate and replacement by another. Quite the contrary: the long history of the unified Chinese state/empire—from the advent of Qin Shi Huangdi's rule in 221 BC to the present day—can be read as a story of the recurrent downfall of established political orders.[5] The Chinese past is fairly littered with deposed dynasties (from 14 to more than 40, depending on who is counting). It scarcely requires a leap in imagination to add one more to that heap.

Some observers of the Chinese scene maintain that the breakdown or overthrow of China's current government system is more than just a theoretical possibility.[6] Instead, they regard it as a likely eventuality. In this telling, the current Chinese order is already in the midst of a lethal systemic crisis, the warning signs of which are said to include rising economic inequalities; mounting social tensions; growing unrest in both rural and urban areas; spreading corruption in government; increasingly cynical and self-interested use of administrative power by government officials; and a populace that increasingly searches for meaning from such philosophical founts as Buddhism, Christianity, and/or Falun Gong—all of which offer value systems that challenge the premises of current Chinese rule. In this exegesis, the crisis of the Chinese system is made still more acute by the growing pressures of pervasive environmental degradation and the precariousness of key aspects of the country's current economic architecture (in particular the banking and financial structure, both of which threaten the economic performance on which Beijing increasingly justifies its authority). Systemic contradictions in this reading are further heightened by an information revolution that is both necessary for enhancing economic performance and subversive of dictatorial control. Although this assessment does not rule out the possibility of international conflict as a precipitating mechanism for a cascade of events leading to the end of Communist governance, the implication is that a collapse will be domestically generated, and may even emanate from within the polity itself.[7]

Even under the very best of circumstances, China's post-1978 economic growth rate will almost surely slow down over the coming generation, simply because the rate of economic expansion over the past three decades has been exceptionally high. From 1978 to 2005, China's estimated GDP growth averaged more than 9 percent a year[8]—a tempo no other economy has ever managed to sustain for more than a few decades.[9]

Despite its spectacular economic performance over the past 30 years, China faces a number of risks in the decades immediately ahead, any one of which could adversely affect productivity and growth. These risks have been widely discussed, but are summarized and reviewed in a 2003 study by the RAND Corporation.[10] They include: 1) spillovers from unemployment, poverty, and social unrest; 2) the economic costs of corruption; 3) setbacks from outbreaks or the spread of epidemic disease, including HIV/AIDS; 4) costs sustained from water shortages and pollution; 5) reverberations from constrained energy supplies or energy price shocks; 6) shockwaves generated by the fragility of the financial system and state-owned enterprises; 7) possible shrinkage of direct foreign investment; and 8) potential international conflict over Taiwan or some other "flashpoint." The RAND study attempts to estimate the growth impact of these various contingencies, and concludes that:

> The probability that none of these individual setbacks will occur is low, while the probability that all will occur is still lower. Were all of them to occur, our estimates indicate that China's growth would be reduced between 7.4 and 10.7 percent annually, thus registering negative numbers for China's economic performance as a whole. While the probability that all will occur is very low, the probability that several will ensue is higher

than their joint probabilities would normally imply. The reason for this multiplication of effect is that their individual probabilities are not independent of one another; the occurrence of one or two will raise the probability that others will ensue. Because of these interdependencies, it is highly likely that several of the separate adversities would tend to cluster if any one of them occurs.[11]

In sum, the study identifies several scenarios that at least plausibly could seriously impinge on, or even curtail, China's economic growth for years to come.

As for the many risks—short of regime change—facing the Chinese state today, the most apparent is the quality and capacity of governance.[12] Although both the state and the Party have met the challenges of maintaining control despite profound and rapid social changes, and have surmounted the hurdles posed by a succession of exacting development policy questions, their record over the past generation may not presage comparable successes in the next. Some observers argue that the next stages of development will require liberalizing the political arena—something the current leadership has neither the disposition nor the ability to deliver.[13] Barring such liberalizations, they warn, the Chinese polity will reveal ever-greater brittleness and vulnerability, conditions that would immediately constrain the mobilization and projection of state power and also darken the prospects for economic growth. Minxin Pei, for example, envisions the possibility that the Chinese system could end up mired in a "trapped transition for an extended period," the consequences of which could include "a prolonged period of stagnation" and "an incapacitated state" replete with "increases in lawlessness, corruption and social disorder."[14] Needless to say, such a China would hardly comport with present expectations for China's economic and political role on the world stage a generation from now. And while such a China would no doubt cause problems for the international community, they would likely be different in scale from those commonly envisioned by strategists and policy planners.

All of the downside contingencies mentioned in the preceding pages could, of course, be fleshed out in greater detail. The difficulty with "alternative futures," however, lies not in adding detail and texture to such scenarios, but in having any presentiment today that such seemingly unlikely visions might actually unfold tomorrow. Simply put, unlike more familiar games of chance, there is no scientific method available to aid the student of Chinese affairs in assigning a probability to the prospect that these "wild cards" will end up being played.[15]

China's Demographic Outlook

Consequential as these Chinese "downsides" could be, we cannot at present assess their likelihood because we have scant basis for reliable long-term political or economic projections. We can be somewhat more confident, however, about relatively long-term projections in one particular realm—demography. Population patterns follow regular and in some ways quite predictable biological rhythms. In a low-mortality and low-fertility setting like contemporary China, one can peer fairly far into the demographic future because relatively little population turnover takes place from one year to the next. Projections by the U.S. Census Bureau make the point: bureau projections anticipate that 78 percent of China's current inhabitants will still be alive in China twenty-three years from now (i.e., 2032) and that 71 percent of that future China's population will be made up of people alive today.[16] The same sort of relatively reliable actuarial techniques that inform today's international life insurance industry permit us to talk with some specificity about the expected population profile of the current Chinese citizenry some twenty-three years hence.

To be sure, there is uncertainty in demographic prognosticating. There is no robust scientific technique for accurate projection of fertility patterns, for example, and the international flow of migration today is determined largely by political decisions rather than natural demographic forces. Even so, barring world-shaking catastrophe, we can hope to have a fair idea of China's population profile in the generation ahead.[17]

With a population of more than 1.3 billion today, China is the world's most populous country—although both U.S. Census Bureau and UN projections anticipate that India will be slightly more populous than China by 2030.[18] Nevertheless, China's total population is expected to continue to grow between now and 2030, although at a steadily slower pace; by the year 2030, China is expected to be a country of nearly 1.5 billion people, approaching zero population growth.

Since migration into and from China has only the most marginal bearing on China's population trends, population change in China is driven by the country's domestic mortality and fertility patterns. Today, China is still a relatively poor country, but it enjoys quite favorable survival patterns, with a life expectancy only a few years lower than those of the affluent countries of the Organization for Economic Cooperation and Development (OECD). In the decades immediately ahead, Chinese life expectancy is assumed to continue to improve modestly. Birth rates in China are very low today: both the UN and the U.S. Census Bureau assume current childbearing patterns are consonant with an average of just 1.7 births per woman per lifetime.[19] This is far below the level necessary for long-term population replacement—about 2.1 births per woman per lifetime—and would imply *ceteris paribus* that each new generation would be more than 20 percent smaller than the one that begat it. Fertility levels are believed to have dropped below the replacement rate in the early 1990s, thanks in part to a coercive anti-natal population control policy that was inaugurated in 1979 and remains in effect at this writing. UN and Census Bureau projections presume that Chinese fertility will remain at sub-replacement levels for the next several decades. In China's major urban centers, fertility levels are even lower, and have been at below replacement rates a decade or so longer than the country as a whole.

Long lives and persistent sub-replacement fertility are not only slowing China's population growth, but radically recasting the country's population structure. In 1980, China's median age was 22 years, with more than twice as many children under the age of 5 as people aged 65 or older. By the year 2005, China's median age had jumped by a decade, to more than 32 years; there are now slightly more senior citizens than young children. By 2030, under current projections, China's median age will be over 41—higher than for Western Europe today, and higher than the projected median age for the U.S. for the year 2030. In this future China, there would be more than three senior citizens for each young child.

China 2030: An Aging and Shrinking Workforce

In a system with essentially zero in-migration, the inexorable consequence of sustained sub-replacement fertility is population aging; as already noted, a massive wave of population aging is in store for China in the generation ahead. Given its pace and scale, China's aging wave might better be described as a tsunami—in the human experience to date, only Japan has undergone a generation of population aging as pronounced and rapid as the one that lies before China today. Two further consequences of this trend are rising old-age dependency ratios (the ratio of retirement-age people to working-age populations) and, eventually, the aging and decline of the working-age population itself. Given current projections, China will be experiencing all of these phenomena in the decades immediately ahead. They could have direct consequences for economic performance, and the consequences are not likely to be favorable.

During its past generation of rapid economic growth, China's development was in a sense abetted by trends in the country's population structure. Between 1980 and 2005, the share of working-age people (those 15 to 64 years of age) in the total population rose substantially, from less than 60 percent to more than 70 percent, while the country's old-age dependency ratio (the ratio of the population aged 65-plus to the working-age population) remained low. Such trends facilitated very high savings and investment rates, which in turn, under the discipline of "outward oriented" economic policies, contributed substantially to China's growth. This dynamic has been described by some economists as a massive "demographic dividend" for China.[20]

But China's demographic dividend has already been cashed, with no more installments pending in the decades ahead. Between now and 2030, China's "dependence ratios" stand to change markedly. Around the year 2010, the ratio of the working-age population to the total population is likely to begin an indefinite decline.

To make matters worse, between today and 2030, China's old-age dependency ratio is set to rise sharply. In 1980, China had 12 working-age people for every man or woman aged 65 and older. Twenty years later, that ratio was still 10 to 1. Today, it is about 9 to 1. By 2030, it may be down to just 4 to 1. Taking into account that not all of the "working-age population" actually works—in China today, a fourth or more of this group is out of the labor force altogether[21]—the dependency and old-age burden implied by these numbers would be even heavier.

The prospective labor force problem, in turn, has absolute and relative aspects. During the past decades of rapid growth, working-age manpower grew substantially. Between 1980 and 2005, for instance, China's working-age population grew by an average of 1.8 percent a year. But working-age population growth is set to peak around the year 2015. Thereafter, China's potential labor force will be characterized by continuing—perhaps accelerating—negative growth. By 2030, China's working-age population could well be smaller than India's.

As China's supply of working-age manpower begins to stagnate or decline, its composition stands to change sharply as well. It is not just Chinese society as a whole that looks to be undergoing rapid aging; the typical Chinese worker will also be much older. At this writing, the median age of Chinese between the ages of 15 and 64 is about 36 years. Under current projections, the corresponding figure for 2030 will be nearly 42 years.

The prospective graying of China's workforce is being driven on the one hand by an expected cresting and diminution in the pool of persons 30 to 44 years of age, and on the other by a precipitous fall-off in the numbers of the population aged 15 to 24. By contrast, China's pool of potential workers from the 50–64 cohort will be growing very rapidly over the generation ahead: by Census Bureau projections, the pace of growth for this cohort will average close to 2 percent a year between 2007 and 2030. From the standpoint of economic performance, the outcome of such workforce aging is not auspicious. To begin, the years 30–44 are a period of unusual creativity and innovation during the course of the life cycle—breakthroughs or discoveries subsequently awarded Nobel Prizes and important patented inventions have disproportionately accrued to people in this age bracket.[22] The absolute and relative decline of this cohort may consequently have implications for inventiveness and creativity in the workforce. For its part, the 15–24 cohort contains the most recently minted graduates of the educational system. And, in our day and age, we can generally expect this group to have both a higher level of educational attainment and a better command of the latest technology than its predecessors. With the drop-off in this youth pool, upgrading the attainment and proficiency of the overall labor force becomes a more difficult challenge, even in purely arithmetic terms. The problem is thrown into relief by the fact that through the 1980s and early 1990s, there were more than three times as many 15- to 24-year-olds as 55- to 64-year-olds. As of 2005, that ratio was still well over 2 to 1. But the ratio is dropping rapidly, and stands to drop further in the decades immediately ahead. By 2020, there will be just about the same number of 15- to 24-year-olds and 55- to 64-year-olds, and by 2030, for every 100 older workers there will only be 77 younger counterparts. The 55 to 64 age group looks to account for a sharply rising share of China's overall workforce in the decades immediately ahead—but it will also be the least-educated and very likely the least-healthy contingent within the labor force.

Viewed in sum, these coming demographic changes stand to exert considerable pressure on China's economic performance. For a generation—from the reformist Third Party Plenum in 1978 until

2005—labor force growth and improvements in human capital contributed an average of about 1.6 percentage points a year to overall GDP growth. But for the period after 2015, the growth in the pool of available manpower looks to be negative, and human capital augmentation looks also to be problematic. By the same token, over the past generation, investment and "capital deepening" (where capital per worker is increasing) are estimated to have contributed about 4 percentage points a year to GDP growth. But with the decline in working-age groups' share in total population and the steady rise in the proportion of senior citizens, the pressure on China's savings rates will progressively mount as well. Just under 4 percentage points a year of GDP growth was attributed to improvements in "total factor productivity," a catch-all category used to reflect changes not directly captured by measures of capital and labor. But with decline in the size and increasing problems in the makeup of the labor force on the one hand, and the downward pressures indicated for investment trends on the other, "total factor productivity" is also likely to be reduced by the demographic changes we have discussed here.

Any Chinese government will attempt to cope with these impending demographic trends, and there is considerable scope for mitigating some of their effects. Not the least of these opportunities would seem to lie in strengthening rules and institutions, especially in the financial sector, intended to improve the efficiency of what remains a tremendously inefficient economic system.[23] But these demographic pressures cannot be ignored: they narrow the realm of the possible in China's economic future—directly, inescapably, and perhaps very consequentially.

Aging China: Poor, Sick, and Unsupported

An impending problem related to the graying of China's population is the matter of old-age support for China's future senior citizens. China's coercive population control program may have succeeded in limiting the country's rising contingent of young people, but its elderly population will be exploding in the years ahead. From 2007 to

2030, more than 90 percent of China's aggregate population growth is projected to occur in the 65-plus grouping; that cohort will likely more than double as a share of total population. Its numbers are expected to swell to roughly 240 million people.

The prospective share of total population of the 65-plus grouping in China in 2030 is by no means unprecedented: in fact, it would be lower than the 2007 fractions for most OECD countries. There is an important difference here, however: the OECD countries grew rich before they grew old. In 2003, China's 65-plus group accounted for 7.4 percent of its population—but when Japan had a comparable proportion of senior citizens in its overall population, its per capita GDP was perhaps two and a half times higher than China's. No country will ever have aged as pervasively at such low income levels as China looks likely to do over the coming generation.

China, of course, is a vast land with plenty of regional variation: the country's provinces are characterized both by notable differences in provincial demographic profiles and tremendous disparities in levels of per capita output. In 2001, for example, local per capita GDP was thirteen times as high in bustling Shanghai as it was in isolated Guizhou. And while there is a broad overall correlation between graying and income levels in China's provinces today, the correspondence is not a tight one. Over the coming two decades, some of China's most dramatic aging trends are set to unfold in some of today's poorest areas. For example, in 2005, Japan reported the world's highest proportion of persons 65 and older, at about 20.6 percent of total population. But by 2025, the 65-plus cohort is projected to account for 21 percent of the total population in one part of China—and that place is not relatively prosperous Beijing or booming Shanghai. Rather, it is Heilongjiang, in China's Manchurian rustbelt, where per capita output in 2001 was just over $1,100, factored on the basis of then-prevailing exchange rates.

Currently, Japan also reports the world's highest median age, at about 43.2 years. Yet by 2025, nine of China's thirty-one provinces and major municipalities are projected to have higher median ages than contemporary Japan: among them, Liaoning (where the exchange-rate-based GDP per capita was around $1,450 in 2001), Jilin (around $925), and Chongqing (less than $690). Purchasing-power-parity adjustments of these exchange-rate-based figures do not alter the basic picture these figures convey. In sum, in just twenty years, large parts of China will have to support very aged populations on low levels of average income.

How will China's elderly population be supported two decades hence? We can fairly confidently surmise that these prospective pensioners will not be supported by the country's existing state pension arrangements. For all the justifiable anxiety about the current health of national pension systems in various OECD countries, the financial disarray of China's official pension apparatus is in a league of its own. The present value of unfunded liabilities is estimated to exceed the country's current GDP. Funded pensions cover only a small minority (one-sixth to one-fourth) of the total Chinese workforce. And despite a decade of high-level policy deliberations in Beijing, there has been no solution put forward by the government to address this problem.[24]

Thus, China's national "pension system" as of 2025 promises today to be more or less the same system that has always provided for the country's elderly and infirm: namely, the family unit. But herein lies a problem: the success of the Chinese government's anti-natal population policy will result in a plummeting ratio of working-age children to elderly parents in the decades ahead. Whereas the average Chinese woman who celebrated her 60th birthday in the early 1990s had borne five children during her lifetime, her counterpart in 2025 will have had fewer than two.

No less important is the fact that over the next twenty years, China's rising cohorts of prospective retirees face a growing "son deficit." In China it is sons, not daughters, on whom the duty to support aged parents customarily falls. In the early 1990s, about 7 percent of China's 60-year-old women had never borne a son. Today, that percentage is about 10 percent. By 2025, the figure will shoot up to roughly 30 percent. Taking both fertility and survival trends into account, it seems likely that a third or more of Chinese women approaching retirement age two decades from now will have no living sons. Just twenty years from now, tens of millions of aged Chinese seeking financial and material help from their children will be competing for resources with their son-in-law's parents, given China's longstanding cultural norm of near-universal marriage for women. With the traditional social-security system of the Chinese family a more fragile construct than at any time in the recent past, and official government pension guarantees limited and problematic, the grim reality is that many elderly Chinese will have to find alternative means of support.

Despite China's tremendous material progress over the half century beginning in 1975, the nation's elderly will face a continuing need to support themselves in old age through their own labor. And here we encounter the second problem associated with China's aging population. China's elderly workers occupy a decidedly unfavorable position in the country's labor force. At the start of the new century, in comparison with China's overall workforce workers 65 or older were six times as likely to be illiterate or semi-literate. They were also much more likely to work in the agricultural sector: in the year 2000, 87 percent of China's elderly workers were in farming.[25] Thus consigned to labor in the low-income sector of the economy with low levels of human capital, China's older labor force provides almost a textbook definition of the working poor.

Despite China's educational advances, its older population will still be disadvantaged in the year 2025. Approximately two-fifths of China's senior citizens will have only a primary school education or less. And, because China's older workers suffer from lower levels of education and training than the general labor force, they are precisely the cohort most directly obliged to rely on physical effort to earn a living. This will hold true tomorrow as well as today.

This brings us to the third problem that defines China's looming aging crisis. In the years ahead, China's senior citizens are not only likely to face mounting pressures to support themselves through paid labor, and not only likely to find that their employment opportunities are principally in low-paying, physically demanding jobs, they are also likely to be less healthy than their counterparts in other countries.

The proposition that the health of senior citizens in China is more tenuous than for older populations in Western countries is not surprising: older people in China have on average been exposed to more health and nutritional risk, and have less scope for preventing and recovering from illness and injury than older people in affluent societies. Consequently, China's citizens live shorter lives than citizens of OECD countries—and their remaining years are more heavily compromised by serious health problems.

China's outlook for population aging, in sum, can be likened to a slow motion humanitarian tragedy already underway. On the current trajectory, the graying of China threatens many tens of millions of future senior citizens with a penurious and uncertain livelihood in an increasingly successful emerging market. The incidence of individual misfortune implied by current trends suggests that impoverished aging may emerge as a major social problem for China in the years ahead, one that will further magnify the social inequalities with which China is already struggling. In short, there is plenty of "downside" economic, social, and political—in China's emerging crisis in old-age support.

The Crisis in China's Family Structure

The impending crisis in old-age support is a feature of a coming revolution in family structure in China—but it is only a single feature of this revolution. The impact on family structure of the coming demographic changes in China is both far-reaching and radical: to oversimplify only slightly, 2,500 years of East Asian family tradition stand to come to an end with the country's rising generation. Why suggest something so sweeping? Quite simply, because current demographic trends are deeply subversive of the Confucian ethos— and prospective trends are more unfavorable still.

According to some demographic reconstructions, fertility was down to 1.7 births per woman as early as 1974 in Beijing, and just

1.5 births per woman in Shanghai in 1973. [26] By the 1990s, fertility levels in these key Chinese urban settings were below one birth per woman,[27] and have evidently remained there since. As a result, Beijing and Shanghai have eerily "under-supported" population structures today. Needless to say, nothing like these contours has ever been seen before in any national capital, much less in any urban agglomerations of more than 10 million people.

The population pyramids in contemporary Shanghai and Beijing speak to a severe and sudden erosion of the traditional East Asian system of extended family relations. With only two successive generations of childbearing patterns like those now prevailing in both Beijing and Shanghai, a new sort of society will be born: a society in which many—maybe most—people no longer have brothers; no longer have sisters; no longer have uncles or aunts or cousins. It would be a setting in which many—perhaps most—young adults would have only direct lineal elders to count as blood relatives.

The withering away of the Chinese family deserves more attention than it has attracted to date. Indeed, the trend could have major implications for social and economic interactions in the East Asian context. The family is one of the critical aspects of social capital in China: family networks provide the *guanxi*, or relationships, of trust that lubricate business dealings in an environment where legal rights are far from certain and formal official guarantees are transient, at best. As Dwight Perkins has noted, these extended trust networks, based on family relationships, have effectively substituted for formal and transparent legal and institutional structures in the East Asian context, facilitating the reduction of risk and transaction costs that so directly helped to fuel the Chinese boom over the past decades. [28]

If and when Chinese family structures atrophy, or if the scope and role of the family is severely attenuated, social and economic life in China will require reliable and sturdy institutional alternatives to perform functions previously assumed by family networks. Given the demographic prospects of the region, those structures and arrangements will have to be developed very quickly: it is not only

Shanghai and Beijing but virtually all the major urban business centers in China that report steep sub-replacement fertility these days.

If the "social capital" and trust relationships that have to date supported economic and social activity in China come under increasing pressure in the years immediately ahead through "the withering away of the family," what would—or could—fill this vacuum? Two very different alternatives come readily to mind.

The first would entail attempting to "get along" within China's existing structures and established practices: which is to say, relying on increasing levels of corruption and arbitrary authoritarianism simply to make things work. This alternative would seem to comport with Minxin Pei's vision of an increasingly sclerotic and economically inefficient authoritarianism in China; presumably, following this path would reinforce and accentuate such tendencies. The alternative and diametrically opposed path would be to develop de facto substitute sources of social capital to compensate for the decline of the family though the development of liberal institutions— including independent courts, open and transparent governance, rule-based financial deliberations, and eventually a system of genuine rule of law.[29]

The second alternative would be consonant with a move toward far-reaching liberalization, and perhaps democratization, in China. And although the implications for growth by choosing this path are far from pre-ordained, one might expect such institution-building to be auspicious for economic performance. On the other hand, such developments would be subversive of Communist Party prerogative and ultimately of Party rule. Hence, it would be easy to understand why the authorities in China today would not wish to embrace this alternative. However, attempting to "muddle through" the crisis in the Chinese family by relying on corruption and coercion runs the risk of continuing and deepening stagnation. In short, both alternatives pose real threats to the existing polity. China's leadership, however, does not have long to decide how it will cope with the rising challenges of changing family structure.

Unnatural Increases in the Sex Ratio at Birth[30]

A final impending aspect of demographic change in China almost takes us into the realm of science fiction. This is the unnatural but increasing disparities between the numbers of baby boys and baby girls born each year—the country's "sex ratios at birth" (SRBs).

Scientific literature on SRBs shows a predictable biological regularity to the proportion of male and female births. This is true of every ethnicity and, so far as can be told, every time and place in recorded history. A sort of rule of thumb emerges: a ratio of 103 boys per 100 girls is low, but not extraordinary; 104 to 105 looks entirely common; and 106 is high, but not biologically impossible. But eyebrows rise when the sex ratio at birth exceeds 106 per 100. Plainly stated, a sex ratio at birth of over 107 boys per 100 girls is utterly improbable. Yet, for more than two decades basic demographic data reported by Beijing's statistical authorities has indicated that the world's largest population is characterized by an unaccountably high sex ratio at birth—and that this unnatural disparity continues to widen ever further.

To this day, China lacks a comprehensive and reliable birth registration system. Nevertheless, the nation's 1964 census reported that the county's sex ratio for all children under 5 years of age was then 105.7 per 100: a reasonable proxy for the actual sex ratio at birth. China's next census, held in 1982, reported a sex ratio at birth of 108.5 per 100. This result, though biologically impossible, proved to be no anomaly: successive Chinese censuses recorded ever more distorted secondary sex ratios. By the 1990 census, the reported sex ratio at birth was over 111 per 100; in the 1995 micro-census, the tally reached over 115. In the most recent census, conducted in November 2000, approximately 120 baby boys were born for every 100 baby girls.

Contemplating these figures, the first question to come to mind is one of accuracy. To begin, China's coercive "one child policy," in effect since 1979, might encourage a pervasive under-counting of baby girls, as parents try to hide newborn daughters so that they gain another chance to sire a son. As Daniel Goodkind of the U.S. Census Bureau has noted, Chinese hospital statistics consistently record a lower sex ratio at birth than the country's official censuses and vital records.[31]

That said, these data problems do not explain away China's SRB trends. China's four censuses since 1980 exhibit a considerable measure of internal consistency on the issue of sex ratio. That is to say, the bizarre ratios reported for infants in one census tend to be reaffirmed for that same cohort at later ages in subsequent population counts. Chinese parents, finally, may indeed conspire en masse to hide their baby daughters so as to circumvent draconian population program strictures, but hiding them becomes distinctly less feasible once those children reach school age. In the 2000 census, the recorded sex ratio for 7-year-olds was over 117. Taking all the evidence into account, we can only conclude that China's "impossible" sex ratios at birth are, in fact, real.

Although Chinese authorities have expressed alarm about rising SRBs, and in recent years have promulgated penalties for sex-selective abortions, thus far such strictures appear to be utterly ineffective. The latest data from the PRC National Bureau of Statistics reports that, as of 2005, the sex ratio for children 4 years of age or younger—that is to say, the group born after the 2000 China census—was up to almost 123.[32] There is no telling how much higher it may go in the years to come. But even if China's SRB eventually does return to more biologically normal levels, a fateful imbalance has already been cast for the life duration of today's children and tomorrow's would-be brides and grooms.

Over the three decades between the years 2000 and 2030, according to UNPD projections, the sex ratio of China's young adults aged 20 to 39 is set to skyrocket, from 106 to nearly 114; by those same projections, the surfeit of men in this age group would nearly double, to around 23 million "surplus men" by the year 2030. If marriage is taken to be a one-on-one lifetime commitment, it would follow that a large and growing portion of China's young males will be "unmarriageable men" in the decades ahead. To the extent that it makes sense to talk of a "marriage market," China's looks to be in extreme and increasing disequilibrium for years to come. The dynamics of this "market," moreover, will have unforgiving ramifications for men who are uneducated and rural. They will make the least attractive providers in the increasingly competitive business of selecting mates. To the extent that "bride price" in China is established by affluent, urban young men, the Chinese countryside—already the setting for the greatest imbalances in sex ratios—will be increasingly denuded of marriageable young women. If China's disgruntled pensioners can be contentious—as they are already proving to be[33]—what are we to expect of masses of able-bodied rural men who realize they have been cheated out of the chance to find a bride and start a family?

It is not unthinkable that the rise of the phenomenon of the "unmarriageable male" may cause an increase in social tensions, if not social turbulence, in China. We do not know how China's future cohorts of young men are to be socialized with no prospect of a settled, stable family life, and no tradition of honorable bachelorhood.

Urbanization and China's "Floating Population"

Although less predictable than the other demographic phenomena described in this chapter, the growing economic divergence between urban and rural areas and the resulting internal migration add another important dimension to the portrait of China's overall demographic health.

Although urban areas are usually magnets for industrialization and foreign investment in developing countries, China's policy of infusing public money into state-owned enterprises (found typically in urban centers) has artificially increased labor demand in cities. As a result, city-dwellers have benefited more from China's economic revolution than their rural counterparts. Furthermore, the current pension system, as meager as it is, basically only exists in China's cities.

The economic dynamism of China's urban sectors has been the

siren's call for rural workers, leading them to ignore the traditional Confucian ethic of staying close to home. According to the UN Population Division, the percent of the Chinese population living in urban areas has doubled since 1980 (from 19.6 percent to 40.4 percent in 2005); by 2030, more than 60 percent of China's population is projected to live in urban areas. In contrast, China's rural regions, which began to shrink in population in the early 1990s, will continue to decline.[34] This amounts to a tremendous—indeed, historically unprecedented—movement of human beings in the years immediately ahead, creating potentially enormous tensions and uncertainties for those migrating, those left behind, and the local and national governments who rule them.

While the internal migration of young workers to urban areas may slow urban population aging, it will at the same time accelerate the aging in the much poorer rural regions. Given the fact that China's rural "pension system" remains dependent on the family unit taking care of aging parents and grandparents, the movement of young workers out of these areas will only exacerbate the problems associated with a growing population of elderly who lack money, education, and adequate healthcare. Remittances from children in the cities might mitigate some of these problems, but remittances will be contingent on the stability of a family structure that is already under increasing pressure.

Equally important, the Chinese household registration system, which was established to control population flows into urban areas, has given rise to a "floating population" of undocumented internal migrants living in the cities. Under the registration system established in the 1950s, migration can only be considered permanent and legal if a household's registration is officially transferred to the new location. However, given the restricted number of transfers issued, especially for those wishing to move to a more desirable location, many migrants remain outside of the official system.

While estimates of the size of the floating population vary, Zai Liang and Zhongdong Ma (using Chinese census data) report it at 7 million in 1978, 22 million in 1990, and 79 million in 2000. While on the whole the floating population comprises 6.3 percent of China's total population, this ratio is as high as 27 percent, 25 percent, and 19 percent in the urban provinces of Shanghai, Guangdong, and Beijing, respectively.[35] The Chinese Ministry of Public Security projects that the floating population will increase to 160 million by 2010, well more than 10 percent of China's population.[36]

With new data from the 2000 Chinese census, Liang and Ma describe the group in more detail. China's floating population is more likely to be male (54 percent) and between the ages of 15 and 44 (82 percent). In comparison with permanent migrants—those who have local housing registration status—the floating population is largely in search of manual labor or business: According to survey data, 70.6 percent of males and 58.5 percent of females cite this as their primary reason for migration. Permanent migrants, on the other hand, are most likely to cite "education or training" as their main motivation (39.9 percent), compared with only 3.9 percent who say they migrate seeking manual labor. The floating population is also less educated than permanent migrants: three-fourths of the former have not graduated from high school, while 60 percent of the latter have a high school degree or higher.[37] While reform efforts have made obtaining local registration status easier in small towns and cities, large city governments continue to favor migrants with relatively high education or the ability to purchase housing. The majority of the floating population possesses neither, and will likely remain outside of the official Chinese system.

While it would have been impossible in the past for an individual who was not officially registered in a location to survive in China's strictly controlled economy, China's market reforms have given rise to a greater number of private firms that operate outside of the system. But because they are working outside of the system, laborers are denied access to certain occupations, housing, pensions, medical care, and often education. There is little doubt, either in the minds of the migrants or the local population they live among, that this "floating population" is being exploited. With their numbers swelling— and likely to continue to do so as long as Beijing refuses to address the distortions caused by the housing registration system and the incentives for local urban governments to look the other way when it comes to local businesses using these workers—China's floating population will almost certainly be an additional source of tension and instability in an already strained system.

Concluding Remarks

The future is always obscure, but there are "alternative futures" for China, plausible destinations that do not comport with the current widely embraced vision of a "rising China." To recognize the plausibility of an end to Communist power in China, or of a series of systemic and debilitating economic crises, or of a sclerosis from a "trapped transition," is not to predict that any of these things will happen. It is simply to recognize that any of them could happen. Unfortunately, there is no reliable method of assigning odds to such highly unexpected outcomes.

This is where demographic analysis steps in. We can confidently talk about population prospects for China over the coming generation—and on the whole, China's demographic outlook over the coming generation is unfavorable, if not strikingly so. Demographic forces promise to put serious pressure on the country's macro-economic performance (labor force and dependency ratios) and micro-economic performance (changing family structure). Social and political tensions will only be heightened by impending waves of un-pensioned seniors and unmarriageable young men.

The implications of demographic trends are fairly mixed in most developing countries or rising powers. What is striking about China is how consistently adverse the changes in demographic trends appear. Although the specific circumstances are different, contemporary China's clouded demographic outlook is quite similar to the Soviet Union's a generation ago. Then, anyone who followed the USSR's population trends knew these Soviet fundamentals were far from positive—yet this seemed to have little impact on the received impression of the Soviet Union as an established and confident power. We know what happened to the Soviet Union. Had we devoted more attention to the Soviets' demographic dilemmas, we may have been less surprised by the outcome. This is not to say that China's demographic dilemmas are hastening the PRC to the USSR's current resting place. It does, however, suggest that neglect of these underpinnings of any plausible "Chinese rise" exposes us to the risk of big surprises in the future. China's continued rise, if it does indeed occur, could be decidedly more qualified than the smart money today seems to think.

NOTES

INTRODUCTION

1. David Lampton, *The Three Faces of Chinese Power: Might, Money, and Minds* (Berkeley, CA: University of California Press, 2008), 4.

2. See Andrew Nathan, "China's Resilient Authoritarianism," *Journal of Democracy* 14, no. 1 (2003): 6–17.

3. See Kellee S. Tsai, *Capitalism without Democracy: The Politics of Private Sector Development in China* (Ithaca, NY: Cornell University Press, 2007) and C. Fred Bergsten, Bates Gill, Nicholas R. Lardy, and Derek Mitchell, *China: The Balance Sheet* (New York: Public Affairs, 2006) for accounts of China today that argue that whatever difficulties the PRC may face today are outweighed by the regime's strengths and its governing party's capacity to adapt and co-opt elites. For a more pessimistic account of the regime's ability to address its problems effectively, however, see Minxin Pei, *China's Trapped Transition: The Limits of Developmental Autocracy* (Cambridge: Harvard University Press, 2006), 214. Precisely because the party is determined to hang on to power above all else, Pei argues that one should not expect a sudden burst of liberalization but rather a slow and debilitating Chinese decline.

4. For a valuable overview of the CCP's own analysis of these events from the perspective of maintaining its power, see David Shambaugh, *China's Communist Party: Atrophy and Adaptation* (Washington, DC: Woodrow Wilson Press, 2008), 41–102.
5. Mark Leonard, *What Does China Think?* (Philadelphia: Public Affairs, 2008), 76, 79.
6. "Politically, the Hu-Wen leadership has done nothing to loosen coercive controls on dissent, the Internet, or other potential challenges to CCP rule. To the contrary, those who hoped that Hu might be a Gorbachev-in-waiting have been sorely disappointed. Since 2005 . . . a general chill has once again affected the intellectual climate." Shambaugh, *China's Communist Party*, 158.
7. "In discussing strategy, PLA leaders and strategists rarely use a Western 'ends-ways-means' construct. Rather, they discuss strategy in terms of 'comprehensive national power' (*zonghe guoli*). Comprehensive national power (CNP) is the concept by which China's strategic planners use qualitative and quantitative variables to evaluate and measure China's standing in relation to other nations. CNP incorporates both soft, internally oriented indicators of strength—e.g., economic prosperity, domestic cohesion, and cultural influence—and hard, externally oriented measures such as the size of a state's nuclear arsenal, territory, military capability, diplomatic influence, and international prestige." U.S. Department of Defense, *Military Power of the People's Republic of China: 2008*, March 3, 2008, 9. Available at: http://www.defenselink.mil/pubs/pdfs/China_Military_Report_08.pdf.

ONE: AMBITION AND ANXIETY

1. Justus D. Doenecke, *The Presidencies of James A. Garfield and Chester A. Arthur* (Lawrence: University Press of Kansas, 1981), 56.
2. This was acknowledged by the Naval Policy Board of 1890. If American security was threatened, the board argued, it was not because other powers were advancing against American interests but because the United States was "certain to reach out and obstruct the interests of foreign nations." David F. Healy, *US Expansionism*:

The Imperialist Urge in the 1890s (Madison: University of Wisconsin Press, 1970), 44.

3. David Shambaugh, *Modernizing China's Military: Progress, Problems, and Prospects* (Berkeley: University of California Press, 2004), 284. As scholars Andrew Nathan and Robert Ross put it, China was and is stronger "than at any other time in the last 150 years." Nathan and Ross, *The Great Wall and the Empty Fortress* (New York: W.W. Norton and Company, 1998), 156.

4. Shambaugh, 67.

5. Chen Zhimin, "Nationalism, Internationalism and Chinese Foreign Policy," *Journal of Contemporary China* 42 (2005): 38.

6. The idea that China should be preeminent in East Asia "remains relatively strong among both elites and ordinary Chinese citizens." Michael D. Swaine and Ashley J. Tellis, *Interpreting China's Grand Strategy: Past, Present, and Future* (Santa Monica: RAND Corporation, 2000), 15.

7. Peter Hays Gries, *China's New Nationalism* (Berkeley: University of California Press, 2004), 51.

8. U.S. Department of Defense, *Military Power of the People's Republic of China*, March 2007, 7. Available at: http://www.defenselink.mil/pubo/pdfo/070303 China Military Power-final.pdf.

9. Avery Goldstein, "Great Expectations: Interpreting China's Arrival," *International Security* 22 (Winter, 1997–1998): 56.

10. Zheng Bijian, "China's 'Peaceful Rise' to Great Power Status," *Foreign Affairs* (September–October 2005): 22.

11. Gries, 70.

12. Jiang Lifeng et al., *ZhongRi guanxi sanlun (Three Essays on Sino-Japanese Relations)*, as quoted by Gries in *China's New Nationalism*, 39.

13. Li Zhengtang, *Why Japan Won't Settle Accounts: A Record of Japanese War Reparations*, as quoted by Gries in *China's New Nationalism*, 39.

14. Gries, 71.

15. Eric Teo Chu Cheow, "Paying tribute to Beijing: An ancient model for China's new power," *International Herald Tribune*, Wednesday, January 21, 2004.

16. Samuel S. Kim, *China's Quest for Security in the Post-Cold War World*

(Carlisle: Strategic Studies Institute of the U.S. Army War College, 1996), 1. Available at: http://www.strategicstudiesinstitute.army.mil/pdffiles/PUB89.pdf.

17. Goldstein, 60.

18. Melvyn Leffler, *A Preponderance of Power: National Security, the Truman Administration, and the Cold War* (Stanford: Stanford University Press, 1992), 58.

19. Andrew J. Nathan and Bruce Gilley, *China's New Rulers: The Secret Files* (New York: New York Review of Books), 206.

20. Samantha Blum, "Chinese Views of U.S. Hegemony," *Journal of Contemporary China* 12 (2003): 259. "But, as another colonel in PLA intelligence put it, 'Just because America's hegemonic behavior is understandable from a historical perspective does not mean it is acceptable.'" David Shambaugh, "China's Military Views the World," *International Security* 24 (2003): 62.

21. David Shambaugh, *Beautiful Imperialist: China Perceives America* (Princeton: Princeton University Press), 226.

22. Samantha Blum, "Chinese Views of U.S. Hegemony," *Journal of Contemporary China* 12 (2003): 239–264.

23. Nathan and Gilley, *China's New Rulers*, 208.

24. The British even left Canada essentially to American mercies, for the British military had no confidence that it could stop a determined United States from conquering it if it really wanted to do so.

25. Yong Deng and Fei-Ling Wang (eds.), *China Rising: Power and Motivation in Chinese Foreign Policy* (Lanham: Rowman and Littlefield, 2005), 10.

26. Blum, 246.

27. Zhang Minqian, "Globalization versus U.S. Strategy," *Contemporary International Relations* 10 (2000): 14.

28. Shambaugh, *Modernizing China's Military*, 298.

29. See Alastair Iain Johnston, "China's International Relations: The Political and Security Dimensions," in Samuel S. Kim (ed.), *The International Relations of Northeast Asia* (Lanham: Rowman and Littlefield, 2003), 73.

30. Yan Xuetong, *Meiguo Baquan yu Zhongguo Anquan [US Hegemony and China's Security]* (Tianjin: Tianjin People's Press, 2000), 23.

31. Shambaugh, *Beautiful Imperialist*, 274.

TWO: CHINA'S GRAND STRATEGY

1. "China's growing pains," *The Economist*, August 19, 2004.

2. John Garver, "Interpreting China's Grand Strategy," *Jamestown Foundation China Brief*, July 5, 2005, 1.

3. The discussion about the Chinese economy and its economic performance thus far is based closely on Angus Maddison, *Chinese Economic Performance in the Long Run*, Second Edition, 960–2030 AD (Paris: OECD, 2007), and Zuliu Hu and Mohsin S. Khan, "Why is China Growing so Fast?," *Economic Issues* 8 (Washington, DC: International Monetary Fund, 1997).

4. Barry R. Posen, *The Sources of Military Doctrine* (Ithaca: Cornell University Press, 1984), 13.

5. Huaqiu Liu, "Discussing Important Period of Strategic Opportunity," *Renmin Ribao*, translation in FBIS CPP20030414000079, April 14, 2003.

6. Edward Luttwak, *The Grand Strategy of the Soviet Union* (New York: St. Martin's Press, 1983), 32.

7. This more recent shift in China's evolving grand strategy—and its details, which are summarized in this section—is usefully surveyed in Evan Medeiros and Taylor Fravel, "China's New Diplomacy," *Foreign Affairs* 82, no. 6 (2003): 22–35, and David Shambaugh, "China Engages Asia: Reshaping the Regional Order," *International Security* 29, no. 3 (Winter 2004–05): 64–99.

8. "Peaceful Rise," *The Economist*, June 24, 2004.

9. For a detailed analysis that examines why alternative phenomena such as economic interdependence, the changing nature of power, the presence of nuclear weapons, and the prospects for a democratic peace pursuant to China's internal transformation would be unlikely to induce China toward something other than assertive international behavior, see Michael D. Swaine and Ashley J. Tellis, *Interpreting China's Grand Strategy* (Santa Monica: RAND Corporation, 2000), 187–217.

10. Maddison, *Chinese Economic Performance in the Long Run*, 93ff.

11. Robert Gilpin, "The Theory of Hegemonic War," *Journal of Interdisciplinary History* 18, no. 4 (1988): 591.

12. Constantine C. Menges, *China: The Gathering Threat* (Nashville: Nelson Current, 2005), 367–417.

13. Chinese Foreign Ministry Spokesperson Qin Gang, press conference at the Embassy of the People's Republic of China in the Republic of Indonesia, September 15, 2005. Available at: http://www.mfa.gov.cn/ce/ceindo/eng/fyrth/t212428.htm.

14. "Strong China 'no threat to Asia,' " *BBC News Online*, April 6, 2005. Available at: http://news.bbc.co.uk/2/hi/south_asia/4412681.stm.

15. John Gerard Ruggie, "Continuity and Transformation in the World Polity: Toward a Neorealist Synthesis," in *Neorealism and its Critics*, ed. Robert O. Keohane (New York: Columbia University Press, 1986), 135.

THREE: DETERRING CHINA

1. Avery Goldstein, "Great Expectations: Interpreting China's Arrival," *International Security* 22, no. 3 (1997/98): 70. For variations of this argument, see Robert S. Ross, "Navigating the Taiwan Strait: Deterrence, Escalation Dominance and U.S.-China Relations," *International Security* 27, no. 2 (2002): 48–85 and Robert S. Ross, "The Stability of Deterrence in the Taiwan Strait," *National Interest*, no. 65 (2001): 67–76.

2. Henry Kissinger, *Diplomacy* (New York: Simon & Schuster, 1994), 608.

3. Colin S. Gray, *Maintaining Effective Deterrence* (Carlisle: Strategic Studies Institute of the U.S. Army War College, 2003), 2.

4. See Fritz W. Ermarth, "Contrasts in American and Soviet Strategic Thought," *International Security* 3, no. 2 (1978): 138–55. Compare with Raymond L. Garthoff, "Mutual Deterrence and Strategic Arms Limitation in Soviet Policy," *International Security* 3, no. 1 (1978): 112–146, and Leon Gouré et al., *The Role of Nuclear Forces in Current Soviet Strategy* (Miami: Center for Advanced International Studies, 1974).

5. John Lewis Gaddis, *The Cold War: A New History* (New York: Penguin Press, 2005), 78.

6. For a fuller account of this phenomenon, see T.V. Paul, *Asymmetric Conflicts: War Initiation by Weaker Powers* (New York: Cambridge University Press, 1994).

7. See Ivan Arreguin-Toft, *How the Weak Win Wars: A Theory of Asymmetric Conflict* (New York: Cambridge University Press, 2005).

8. Colin S. Gray, *Maintaining Effective Deterrence* (Carlisle: Strategic Studies Institute of the U.S. Army War College, 2003), 13.

9. Ibid., 32.

10. Fred Charles Iklé, "Nuclear Strategy: Can There Be a Happy Ending?" *Foreign Affairs* 63, no. 4 (1985): 10.

11. Gray, 32.

12. Quoted in Robert Jervis, "Deterrence Theory Revisited," *World Politics* 31, no. 2 (1979): 306, a review of *Deterrence in American Foreign Policy: Theory and Practice*, by Alexander George and Richard Smoke.

13. Richard K. Betts, *Surprise Attack* (Washington, DC: The Brookings Institution, 1982), 47.

14. Henry Kissinger, *Years of Upheaval* (New York: Little Brown & Co, 1982), 460 and 465.

15. Paul, 132.

16. Ibid, 150–52.

17. Blumenthal, Dan. "Fear and Loathing in Asia," *Journal of International Security Affairs* 59, no. 2 (2006).

18. Arguably, dissuasion has not worked. China is competing with the United States in space, cyber, and naval warfare.

19. For a summary of this argument, see Alastair Iain Johnston, *Cultural Realism: Strategic Culture and Grand Strategy in Chinese History* (Princeton, NJ: Princeton University Press, 1995), 63–65.

20. Ibid., 27.

21. Alastair Iain Johnston, "China's Militarized Interstate Dispute Behavior: 1949–1992: A First Cut at the Data," *The China Quarterly* 153 (1998): 27–29. Quoted in Michael D. Swaine and Ashley J. Tellis, *Interpreting China's Grand Strategy: Past, Present, and Future* (Santa Monica: RAND Corporation, 2000), 47.

22. See Abram N. Shulsky, *Deterrence Theory and Chinese Behavior* (Santa Monica: RAND Corporation, 2000), 75.

23. Huiyun Feng, *Chinese Strategic Culture and Foreign Policy Decision-Making: Confucianism, Leadership, and War* (New York: Routledge, 2007), 68 and 72.

24. Shulsky, 14. For other accounts, see Allen S. Whiting, "China's Use of Force, 1950–96, and Taiwan," *International Security* 26, no. 2 (2001): 103–131. See also Andrew Scobell, *China's Use of Military Force: From the Great Wall to the Long March* (Cambridge: Cambridge University Press, 2003), 123–130. Scobell makes the point that China's use of force was an emotional reaction to the mistreatment of ethnic Chinese, and to general "anti-Chinese" behavior.

25. Regarding the Chinese intervention in the Korean War, T.V. Paul writes: "the legitimacy of the new regime was also in question given the precarious nature of its position internally. According to one Chinese historian, if China gave in to the US, the Communist Party would have lost the support of the people. . . . This was evident in Mao's message on October 12, 1950 to Zhou En-lai who was in Moscow: 'If we adopt a policy of non-intervention and let our enemy to press the bank of Yalu river, the reactionary arrogance inside and outside the country will be inspired' . . . removing the external threat became imperative for the regime's internal legitimacy and control." *Asymmetric Conflicts*, 103–04.

26. Alexander L. George, "'Operational Code': A Neglected Approach to the Study of Political Leaders and Decision-making," *International Studies Quarterly* 13, no. 2 (1969), 197.

27. Thomas J. Christensen, *Useful Adversaries: Grand Strategy, Domestic Mobilization, and Sino-American Conflict, 1947–1958* (Princeton, NJ: Princeton University Press, 1996), 93.

28. "In the summer of 2004, there were reports of policy conflict between Jiang on the one side, and Hu Jintao and Wen Jiabao on the other. Most observers concluded, however, that the toughening of the Chinese position was primarily a response to what the Chinese regarded as a deteriorating situation and secondarily an effort by Jiang to reaffirm his authority as CMC chairman." Richard Bush, "Chinese Decisionmaking Under Stress: The Taiwan Strait, 1995–2004," in *Chinese National Security: Decisionmaking Under Stress*, eds. Andrew Scobell and Larry M. Wortzel (Carlisle: Strategic Studies Institute of the U.S. Army War College, 2005), 148.

29. Cheng Li, "China's Road Ahead: Will the New Generation of Leaders Make a Difference?" *Brown Journal of World Affairs* 9, no. 1 (2002): 337.

30. Quoted in Shulsky, 21.

31. Susan Shirk, *China: Fragile Superpower: How China's Internal Politics Could Derail Its Peaceful Rise* (Oxford: Oxford University Press, 2007), 47.

32. "China sub secretly stalked U.S. fleet; Surfaced within torpedo range of aircraft carrier battle group," *Washington Times,* November 13, 2006, A1.

33. "Japan and China face off over energy," *Asia Times,* July 2, 2005.

34. Robert Sutter, "The PLA, Japan's Defense Posture, and the Outlook for China-Japan Relations," in *Shaping China's Security Environment: The Role of the People's Liberation Army,* ed. Andrew Scobell and Larry M. Wortzel (Carlisle: Strategic Studies Institute of the U.S. Army War College, 2006), 182.

35. Michael D. Swaine, "Understanding the Historical Record" in *Managing Sino-American Crises: Case Studies and Analysis,* eds. Michael D. Swain, Zhang Tuosheng, and Danielle F.S. Cohen (Washington, DC: Carnegie Endowment for International Peace, 2006), 12.

36. Ibid.

37. See Shirk, *Fragile Superpower,* Chapter 7 ("Taiwan: A Question of Regime Survival").

38. Swaine and Tellis, 38. See also, Frederick W. Mote, *Imperial China. 900–1800* (Boston: Harvard University Press, 2000), 849.

39. Harry Gelber, *The Dragon and the Foreign Devils: China and the World, 1100 BC to the Present* (New York: Walker & Company, 2007), 211, and Jonathan D. Spence, *The Search for Modern China* (New York: W.W. Norton & Co, 1990), 223.

40. Shu Guang Zhang, *Deterrence and Strategic Culture: Chinese-American Confrontations, 1949–1958* (Ithaca, NY: Cornell University Press, 1992), 55.

41. Zhang, 74.

42. Quoted in John Wilson Lewis and Litai Xue, *Imagined Enemies: China Prepares for Uncertain War* (Stanford, CA: Stanford University Press, 2006), 261.

43. For background on the evolution of the Clinton Administration's China policy in the face of China's growing military weight, see Barton Gellman, "U.S. and China Nearly Came to Blows in '96," *Washington Post,* June 21, 1998, A1, and Gellman, "Reappraisal

Led to New China Policy," *Washington Post,* June 22, 1998, A1. As a result of that reappraisal, on President Clinton's June 1998 visit to China he stated his "three no's" policy—no U.S. support for a two-China policy, Taiwan's independence, or even Taipei's membership in international organizations for which statehood is required.

44. This inclination culminated in President Bush's statement on December 9, 2003, chastising President Chen's "unilateral" actions. "President Bush and Wen Jiabao Remarks to the Press," The White House, December 9, 2003. Available at: http://www.whitehouse.gov/news/releases/2003/12/20031209-2.html.

45. "Not long before the [March 1996] missile firings, in January, a former Clinton administration defense official had reported to [then NSC Advisor Anthony] Lake on a disquieting set of conversations he had held in Beijing. Chas. W. Freeman Jr. was a China specialist who served as President Richard Nixon's interpreter in Beijing in 1972 and most recently as assistant secretary of defense. In arguments over Taiwan with top Chinese military officials . . . he said he had heard an implied nuclear threat against the United States. 'I said you'll get a military reaction from the United States' if China attacks Taiwan, Freeman recalled, 'and they said, "No, you won't. We've watched you in Somalia, Haiti and Bosnia, and you don't have the will."' Then, according to Freeman, a senior officer added: 'In the 1950s, you three times threatened nuclear strikes on China, and you could do that because we couldn't hit back. Now we can. So you are not going to threaten us again because, in the end, you care a lot more about Los Angeles than Taipei.'" Gellman, "U.S. and China Nearly Came to Blows in '96."

46. Huang Shi Gong's *San Lue* (Three Tactics), one of the *Seven Military Classics* (Sun Tzu's *The Art of War* is also included in the collection), insists that the weak can beat the strong by adopting a more compliant posture. Alastair Iain Johnston, *Cultural Realism: Strategic Culture and Grand Strategy in Chinese History* (Princeton, NJ: Princeton University Press, 1995), 134. This concept is also present in the Taoist notion that one should use "weakness to overcome strength" and "softness to overcome hardness." Ibid., 119.

47. Barry R. Posen, *The Sources of Military Doctrine: France, Britain, and Germany Between the World Wars* (Ithaca, NY: Cornell University

Press, 1984), 15. At the outbreak of World War II, the entire Swiss nation mobilized within three days, the fighting force eventually numbering 850,000 people out of 4 million. As the Nazis prepared invasion plans, the Swiss shifted from a static defense to a strategy of a long, cost-imposing war of attrition, organizing all able-bodied men into local civil defense units and ordering those who might confront invading Germans to fire "even if they find themselves completely alone." The Germans preparing invasion plans commented on the problem of a heavily armed country with a reputation for stellar marksmanship. While there are many reasons why the Germans did not invade Switzerland, the Swiss mastery of mobilization and civil defense certainly factored into Nazi calculations. See Stephen P. Halbrook, "Citizens in Arms: The Swiss Experience," *Texas Review of Law and Politics* 8, no. 1 (2003): 164–166. Also, Laurent Michaud, "Swiss Armed Forces and the Challenges of the 21st Century," *Military Review* (September-October 2004): 89.

48. Chinese scholars Zhu Liangyin and Meng Renzhong from the Academy of Military Science (AMS) represent this view well in saying that "military power is critical in ensuring that economic power will rise, protecting the nation's general interests, and carrying out global strategic goals," identifying military power as key to Comprehensive National Power. Michael Pillsbury, *China Debates the Future Security Environment* (Washington, DC: National Defense University Press, 2000), 210.

FOUR: JAPAN'S RESPONSE TO THE RISE OF CHINA

1. See Michael R. Auslin, *Negotiating with Imperialism: The Unequal Treaties and the Culture of Japanese Diplomacy* (Cambridge: Harvard University Press, 2004); and William G. Beasley, *Japanese Imperialism 1894–1945* (New York: Oxford University Press, 1999).

2. *Sui shu* (Peking: Chung-hua, 1973), 81.1827, quoted in Wang Zhenping, "Speaking with a Forked Tongue: Diplomatic Correspondence between China and Japan, 238–608 A.D.," *Journal of the American Oriental Society* 114, no. 1 (1994): 29.

3. Wayne M. Morrison, "China-U.S. Trade Issues," *Congressional Research Service Report*, May 3, 2007.

4. Statistics from Japan External Trade Organization, "Japanese Trade in 2005," June 2006, 187. Available at: http://www.jetro.go.jp/jpn/reports/05001265, and Axel Berkofsky, "Sino-Japanese Relations Recovering," *Energy Publisher*, June 20, 2007. Available at: http://www.energypublisher.com/article.asp?idarticle=10006.

5. "Japanese Trade in 2005," 164.

6. For two examples, see Jason Dean, "The Forbidden City of Terry Gou," *Wall Street Journal*, August 11, 2007, and Ian Rowley, "Toyota in China: Full Speed Ahead," *Business Week*, March 9, 2007. Toyota was producing the Prius in China for the domestic Chinese market, of which the Japanese currently have a miniscule share.

7. Akio Takahara, "Integration versus Confrontation: The Complexity of Sino-Japanese Relations," *Sasekawa Peace Foundation*, November 29, 2005, available at: http://www.spfusa.org/Program/av2005/112905.pdf

8. Figures from Japan External Trade Organization, "Japan's Outward FDI (based on reports and notifications) by Country/Region." Available: at http://www.jetro.go.jp/en/stats/statistics/rnfdi_01_e.xls.

9. "Japanese Trade in 2005," 103.

10. See, for example, Warren I. Cohen, *East Asia at the Center* (New York: Columbia University Press, 2000), and Mark Mancall, *China at the Center: 300 Years of Foreign Policy* (New York: Free Press, 1984).

11. Chinese figures from GlobalSecurity.org, "People's Liberation Navy-Personel," August 7, 2007, available at: http://www.globalsecurity.org/military/world/china/plan-personel.htm, Japanese figures from Japan Ministry of Defense, "Authorized and Actual Numbers of the Self-Defense Personnel," March 31, 2006. Available at: http://www.mod.go.jp/e/data/data12.html.

12. Figures from U.S. Department of Defense, *Military Power of the People's Republic of China*, March 2007, 25. Available at: http://www.defenselink.mil/pubs/pdfs/070523-China-Military-Power-final.pdf.

13. Japanese Ministry of Defense, *Defense of Japan 2007*. Available at: www.mod.go.jp/e/data/data02.html.

14. The *Kitty Hawk* was replaced by the USS *George Washington* in 2008, the first nuclear-powered aircraft carrier to be deployed to Japan.

15. Japan Ministry of Defense, *Defense of Japan 2007*, 2007, Part I,

Chapter 2, Section 3. Available at: http://www.mod.go.jp/e/publ/w_paper/index.html.

16. Ibid., 21.

17. *Defense of Japan 2007*, Part II, Chapter 1, Section 3.

18. *Defense of Japan 2007*, Part II, Chap. 1, 4. The three non-nuclear principles include not possessing nuclear weapons, not producing nuclear weapons, and not allowing nuclear weapons in Japan.

19. For a discussion of this change in Japan's defense posture, see Christopher Griffin and Dan Blumenthal, "Japan: A Liberal, Nationalistic Defense Transformation," *Asian Outlook*, American Enterprise Institute, October 2005. Available at: http://www.aei.org/publications/pubID.23464/pub_detail.asp.

20. GlobalSecurity.org, "F-15J," November 14, 2006. Available at: http://www.globalsecurity.org/military/world/japan/f-15j.htm.

21. "First Boeing KC-767 Tanker for Japan Begins Test Readiness Review," *Boeing News Release*, July 18, 2006. Available at: http://www.boeing.com/ids/news/2006/q3/060717i_nr.html.

22. "F-22 Raptors to Japan?" *Defense Industry Daily*, July 15, 2005. Available at: http://www.defenseindustrydaily.com/f22-raptors-to-japan-01909.

23. The Shanghai Cooperation Organisation, "History of development of Shanghai Cooperation Organisation," Available at: http://www.sectsco.org/html/00035.html.

24. U.S. Department of State, "Joint Statement of the U.S.-Japan Security Consultative Committee," February 19, 2005. Available at: http://www.state.gov/r/pa/prs/ps/2005/42490.htm.

25. See, for example, Anthony Faiola, "Japan-Taiwan Ties Blossom as Regional Rivalry Grows," *Washington Post*, March 24, 2007.

26. It should be noted, however, that Japan has not repeated this concern about Taiwan. Subsequent SCC statements (2006 and 2007), made no reference to Taiwan. Instead, Washington and Tokyo recognized "the importance of China's contributions to regional and global security." This has been reinforced by Tokyo's desire to calm relations with Beijing, both for better relations in and of themselves and to give Tokyo a freer hand in asserting itself regionally and globally.

FIVE: FACING REALITIES

1. *Mapping the Global Future: Report of the National Intelligence Council's 2020 Project* (Washington, DC: National Intelligence Council, 2004), 47. Available at: http://www.dni.gov/nic/ NIC_globaltrend2020_s2.html.

2. The U.S. is also a member of the ASEAN Regional Forum (ARF), established in 1994. But its diversity of membership (now consisting of 27 participants) and "lowest-common-denominator" approach to addressing security issues has resulted in Washington taking far less interest in the forum than either APEC or the Six-Party Talks. See Akikio Fukushima, "The Asian Regional Forum," in *The Regional Organizations of the Asia-Pacific: Exploring Institutional Change*, ed. Michael Wesley (Basingstroke: Plagrave Macmillan, 2003), 76–95.

3. On the Clinton Administration's vision for a fellowship of Asian democracies, see President Bill Clinton's speech titled "Building a New Pacific Community" at Waseda University, Tokyo, Japan, on July 7, 1993. The speech is available at: http://findarticles. com/p/articles/mi_m1584/is_n28_v4/ai_13238867. For the Bush Administration's vision, see *The National Security Strategy of the United States of America* (Washington, DC: Government Printing Office, 2002): 25–26, and candidate Bush's statement during the 2000 campaign that the U.S. should "work toward the day when the fellowship of free Pacific nations is as strong and united as our Atlantic partnership." George W. Bush, "A Distinctly American Internationalism" (Reagan Presidential Library, Simi Valley, California, November 19, 1999). Available at: http://www.mtholyoke. edu/acad/intrel/bush/wspeech.htm.

4. Daniel Twining, "America's Grand Design in Asia," *The Washington Quarterly* 30, no. 3 (2007): 80.

5. The Treaty of Rome was signed by France, West Germany, Italy, Belgium, the Netherlands, and Luxembourg on March 25, 1957; it established the European Economic Community (EEC), an independent supranational economic organization. It was subsequently modified by the Treaty of Maastricht (1992), which established the European Community (TEC) and the European Union.

6. The charter's text can be found at: http://www.aseansec.org/ASEAN-Charter.pdf.

7. David Martin Jones and Michael L.R. Smith, "Making Process, Not Progress," *International Security* 32, no. 1 (2007): 182.

8. Ralph Cossa, "One (very) Small Step Forward for ASEAN," *The Japan Times*, November 26, 2007.

9. See Evelyn Goh, "Great Powers and Hierarchical Order in Southeast Asia," *International Security* 32, no. 3 (Winter 2007–2008): 113–57 and Alice D. Ba, "Who's Socializing Whom? Complex Engagement in Sino-ASEAN Relations," *Pacific Review* 19, no. 2 (2006): 157–79.

10. For background on this relationship and prospects for this socialization thesis, see Jing-dong Yuan, *China-ASEAN Relations: Perspectives, Prospects and Implications for U.S. Interests*, (Carlisle: Strategic Studies Institute of the U.S. Army War College, 2006); Cheng Chwee Kuik, "Multilateralism in China's ASEAN Policy," *Contemporary Southeast Asia* 27, no. 1 (2005); and Alastair Iain Johnston, "Is China a Status Quo Power?," *International Security* 27, no. 4 (2003): 5–56.

11. Carlyle A. Thayer, "Southeast Asian Reactions to China's Peaceful Development Doctrine: Indonesia, the Philippines, and Thailand" in *Assessing Regional Reactions to China's Peaceful Development Doctrine*: *NBR Analysis* 18, no. 5 (2008), 13.

12. Jones and Smith, 178–79.

13. See, for example, Ian Bremmer, Choi Sung-hong, and Yoriko Kawaguchi, "A New Forum for Peace," *National Interest* 82 (Winter 2005–2006): 107–12, and Michael Schiffer, "Time for a Northeast Asian Security Institution," *PacNet* 59, December 8, 2006. Available at: http://www.csis.org/component/option,com_csis_pubs/task,view/id,3638/type,3/.

14. See remarks by Deputy Secretary John Negroponte to the U.S. Asia Pacific Council on April 11, 2008. "The Six-Party Talks bring together North Korea's neighbors and key regional players on an issue with overlapping interests and a clear, focused purpose: denuclearization of the Korean Peninsula. While the process of denuclearization is far from complete, we hope an eventual peace and security mechanism for Northeast Asia will form to

institutionalize the security cooperation we are forging through the Six Party process." The remarks are available at: http://www.state. gov/s/d/2008/103464.htm.

15. Of course, after the fall of the Soviet Union, the CSCE transformed itself into a more pro-active organization, the OSCE. But with transformation of the Russian state into a pseudo-democracy, the OSCE's ability to act in such a fashion has come to a virtual halt.

16. John S. Park, "Inside Multilateralism: The Six-Party Talks," *Washington Quarterly* 28, no. 4 (2005): 75–91.

17. See Michael R. Auslin, "Moving Backward in East Asia," *The American*, April 23, 2008.

18. A Northeast Asia security forum would also, if membership were kept to the original five or six states of the Six-Party Talks, potentially make South Korea a kind of "swing" state, subtly accelerating the problems that now exist in U.S.-Republic of Korea relations.

19. The East Asian Summit consists of the ten member states of ASEAN as well as Japan, South Korea, China, India, Australia, and New Zealand. The first annual summit was held in Kuala Lumpur, Malaysia, on December 14, 2005. Russia has applied for membership.

20. ASEAN Plus Three consists of the ten member states of ASEAN plus Japan, South Korea, and China. The first meeting was held in 1997, with the convening of the leaders of ASEAN and their counterparts from China, Japan, and South Korea on the sidelines of an ASEAN summit in Malaysia. The primary driver behind the meeting was that year's Asian financial crisis. The result of the meeting was the Chiang Mai Initiative, a plan to create a network of central banks from the thirteen countries designed to manage regional short-term liquidity problems by facilitating swaps in reserves. ASEAN Plus Three was institutionalized in 1999. The Shanghai Cooperation Organization is made up of six member states: China, Russia, Kazakhstan, Kyrgyzstan, Tajikistan, and Uzbekistan. Iran has also applied for membership. Since 1996, the organization has signed a number of agreements in the areas of border security and counterterrorism, engaged in military exercises, and broadened cooperation in the areas of economics and energy. In

2001, in St. Petersburg, the members signed the SCO Charter, which set out the organization's structure, purposes, and form of operation.

21. Daniel Twining, "Asia's Challenge to China," *Financial Times*, September 25, 2007, and Shulong Chu, "The East Asia Summit: Looking for an Identity," *Brookings Northeast Asia Commentary*, February 1, 2007. Available at: http://www.brookings.edu/ opinions/2007/02northeastasia_chu.aspx.

22. Hongying Wag, "Multilateralism in Chinese Foreign Policy: The Limits of Socialization," *Asian Survey* 40, no. 3 (2000): 485–86.

23. Both the Philippines and Thailand have formal alliances with the United States and both have been designated by Washington as a "major non-NATO ally."

24. Nick Bisley, "Asian Security Architectures" in *Strategic Asia 2007–08: Domestic Political Change and Grand Strategy*, eds. Ashley J. Tellis and Michael Wills (Washington, D.C.: The National Bureau of Asian Research, 2007), 348.

25. APEC's 21 member economies are Australia; Brunei Darussalam; Canada; Chile; the People's Republic of China; Hong Kong, China; Indonesia; Japan; the Republic of Korea; Malaysia; Mexico; New Zealand; Papua New Guinea; Peru; the Republic of the Philippines; the Russian Federation, Singapore, Chinese Taipei, Thailand, the United States of America; and Vietnam. It was established in 1989 to enhance economic growth in the Asia-Pacific community. India has asked to become a member.

26. C. Raja Mohan, "Poised for Power: The Domestic Roots of India's Slow Rise," *Strategic Asia 2007–08: Domestic Political Change and Grand Strategy*, eds. Ashley J. Tellis and Michael Wills (Washington, D.C.: The National Bureau of Asian Research, 2007), 204.

27. Bisley, 342.

28. Ralph A. Cossa, "East Asia Community Building: Time for the United States to Get on Board," *Stanley Foundation Policy Analysis Brief*, September 2007. Available at: http://www.stanleyfoundation. org/publications/pab/CossaPAB07.pdf.

29. Comments delivered at the International Institute for Strategic Studies Conference on East Asia Security, Foreign Press Center Building, Washington, D.C., May 29, 2002. Available at: http://fpc.

state.gov/fpc/10566.htm. See also, Christopher Hemmer and Peter Katzenstein, "Why is There No NATO in Asia? Collective Identity, Regionalism, and the Origins of Multilateralism," *International Organization* 56, no. 3 (2002): 575–607.

30. The text of the Final Act is available at: http://www.osce.org/documents/mcs/1975/08/4044_en.pdf.

31. See note 133 above for link to the text of the charter.

32. "In subtle ways, people across East Asia, like Europeans after World War II, are beginning to think of themselves as citizens of a region." Joshua Kurlantzick, "Pax Asia-Pacifica? East Asian Integration and Its Implications for the United States," *Washington Quarterly* 30, no. 3 (2007): 68.

33. Bisley, 349.

34. Robert Albritton and Thawilwadee Bureekul, "Social and Cultural Supports for Plural Democracy in Eight Asian Nations: A Cross-National, Within-Nation Analysis," *Asian Barometer Working Paper Series*, no. 31 (2005). Available at: http://www.asianbarometer.org/newenglish/publications/workingpapers/no.31.pdf. See also Paul Wiseman, "Asian Nations Cultivate New Sense of Democracy," *USA Today*, March 13, 2008.

35. For an overview of these trends see Michael J. Green, "Democracy and the Balance of Power in Asia," *American Interest* (September/October 2006): 95–102; Daniel Twining, "America's Grand Design in Asia," *Washington Quarterly* 30, no. 3 (2007): 79–94, and "Strong Backing for India's Inclusion in Security Arrangement," *Press Trust of India*, March 15, 2007.

36. *The National Security Strategy of the United States of America* (Washington, DC: Government Printing Office, 2002): 1.

37. Daniel Twining, "Playing the America Card," *Weekly Standard*, October 1, 2007.

38. See Francis Fukuyama, "The Security Architecture in Asia and American Foreign Policy," in *East Asian Multilateralism: Prospects for Regional Stability*, eds. Kent E. Calder and Francis Fukuyama (Baltimore: Johns Hopkins University Press, 2008), 249.

39. For the most famous, modern statement of the "democratic peace theory," see Michael W. Doyle, "Kant, Liberal Legacies, and Foreign Affairs, Part I," *Philosophy and Public Affairs* 12, no. 3 (1983): 205–35.

SIX: THE RISE OF TAIWAN

1. Secretary of State Condoleezza Rice, "Press Briefing on the President's Visit to China" (China World Hotel, Beijing, PRC. November 20, 2005). Available at: http://www.state.gov/secretary/rm/2005/57412.htm.

2. Richard C. Bush, *At Cross Purposes: U.S.-Taiwan Relations Since 1942* (Armonk, NY: M.E. Sharpe, 2004), 124.

3. Ibid. The 1972 communiqué stated the "United States acknowledges that all Chinese on either side of the Taiwan Strait maintain there is but one China and that Taiwan is a part of China." The 1979 communiqué established U.S.-PRC relations. The 1982 communiqué stated that it was Washington's intention to gradually reduce arms sales to Taiwan. In the case of the last communiqué, however, President Reagan placed a memorandum in the National Security Council files that stated that U.S. willingness to reduce its arms sales to Taiwan would be conditioned on the commitment of China to the peaceful solution of the cross-strait issue. For an extended discussion of the communiqués, see Bush, 125ff.

4. Charles Babington and Dana Milbank, "Bush Advisers Try to Limit Damage; No Change in Policy Toward Taiwan," *The Washington Post*, April 27, 2001, A19.

5. See "United States-People's Republic of China: Joint Communiqué [Shanghai Communiqué]," *U.S. Department of State Bulletin* 66 (1972): 435, issued in Shanghai on February 27, 1972.

6. Margaret MacMillan, *Nixon and Mao: The Week That Changed the World* (New York: Random House, 2007), 256–260.

7. MacMillan, 260.

8. Bush, 134.

9. Bush, 128.

10. The "three no's" are: No support for Taiwan's independence; no support for two Chinas; no support for Taiwan membership in the United Nations. See Shirley A. Kahn, "China/Taiwan: The Evolution of the 'One China' Policy—Key Statements from Washington, Beijing, and Taipei," *Congressional Research Service Report for Congress* (July 9, 2007), 9. Available at: http://www.fas.org/sgp/crs/row/RL30341.pdf.

11. James H. Mann, *About Face: A History of America's Curious*

Relationship with China, from Nixon to Clinton (New York: Vintage Books, 1998), 48.

12. This paper uses the term "identity," which is most commonly used among American observers, to refer to the concept that, in Taiwan, is often referred to as "Taiwan consciousness." Mily Ming-Tzu Kao draws out the difference between "identity" and "consciousness" in "The Referendum Phenomenon in Taiwan: Solidification of Taiwan Consciousness," *Asian Survey* 44 (2004): 592, where she argues that the former relates to the identity of the individual and the latter to that of the people as a whole. This paper, however, does not depend on that distinction.

13. Alan M. Wachman, *Taiwan: National Identity and Democratization* (Armonk: M.E. Sharpe, 1994), 91–92.

14. June Teufel Dreyer, "Taiwan's Evolving Identity," *The Evolution of a Taiwanese National Identity: Asia Program Special Report*, no. 114, Woodrow Wilson International Center for Scholars (August 2003): 4.

15. Stephen Phillips, "Building a Taiwanese Republic: The Independence Movement, 1945–Present," in *Dangerous Strait: The U.S.-Taiwan-China Crisis*, ed. Nancy Bernkopf Tucker (New York: Columbia University Press, 2005): 47.

16. Daniel C. Lynch, "Taiwan's Self-Conscious Nation-Building Project," *Asian Survey* 44, no. 4 (2004): 513–514.

17. Denny Roy, *Taiwan: A Political History* (Ithaca, NY: Cornell University Press, 2003), 37.

18. Wachman, 94.

19. P'eng Ming-min, *A Taste of Freedom: Memoirs of a Formosan Independence Leader* (New York: Holt, Rinehart & Winston, 1972), 51–52. See also George Kerr, *Formosa Betrayed* (Boston: Houghton Mifflin, 1965), 98–99.

20. Wachman, 95.

21. Ibid., 111.

22. Ibid., 96.

23. Ibid., 100–01.

24. Thomas B. Gold, "Identity and Symbolic Power in Taiwan," in *The Evolution of a Taiwanese National Identity: Asia Program Special Report*, no. 114, Woodrow Wilson International Center for Scholars (August 2003): 11.

25. Vincent Wei-cheng Wang, "How Chen Shui-bian Won: The 2004 Taiwan Presidential Election and Its Implications," *Journal of International Security Affairs*, no. 7 (2004): 36.

26. Lynch, 516.

27. Lee Teng-hui, "Understanding Taiwan; Bridging the Perception Gap," *Foreign Affairs* 78, no. 6 (1999): 9.

28. Bruce Jacobs and I-hao Ben Liu, "Lee Teng-Hui and the Idea of Taiwan," *The China Quarterly*, no. 190 (2007): 388. For more on Lee's role in promoting Taiwanese national identity, see pp. 375–393.

29. Gunther Schubert, "Taiwan's Political Parties and National Identity: The Rise of an Overarching Consensus," *Asian Survey* 44, no. 4 (2004).

30. Melissa J. Brown, *Is Taiwan Chinese: The Impact of Culture Power and Migration on Changing Identities* (Berkeley: University California Press, 2004), 12.

31. Jason Dean, "National Identity Grows in Taiwan," *Asian Wall Street Journal*, March 1, 2004, A1.

32. Ibid. According to the National Chengchi Poll, that number fell slightly from 1993 (45.4 percent) to 2004 (43.8 percent).

33. Schubert, 537. See also Shelley Rigger, "Disaggregating the Concept of National Identity," *Asia Program Special Report*, no. 114, Woodrow Wilson International Center for Scholars (August 2003): 17.

34. "Ma Declares Future of Taiwan Should Not Be Decided by China," *Taiwan News*, Oct. 16, 2007. KMT presidential candidate Ma said that "it ought to be up to the people of Taiwan to decide the nation's future, no matter what decision they arrive at." See also, "Ma Offers Alternative View on Relations with China," Editorial, *China Post*, Feb. 16, 2006: "Regarding Taiwan's future, Ma does not rule out eventual unification with the Chinese mainland as an option. Yet he said that such integration can be realized only when the mainland has developed into a country with democratic, economic and social progress reaching Taiwan's levels."

35. "DPP, KMT vow to press on with UN referendum bids," *Taipei Times*, September 2, 2007, 3.

36. Schubert, 535.

37. Lynch, 514.

38. Michael Gonzalez, "Chen's Identity Politics Limits Taiwanese Freedoms," *Asian Wall Street Journal*, March 17, 2004, A7.
39. Rigger, 19.
40. Ibid.
41. Ibid., 2.
42. Ibid., 20.
43. Schubert, 537.
44. Ibid.
45. Nancy B. Tucker, *Taiwan, Hong Kong and the United States, 1945–1992: Uncertain Friendships* (New York: Twayne Publishers, 1994), 77.
46. John W. Garver, *Face off: China, the United States and Taiwan's Democratization*, (Seattle: University of Washington Press, 1997), 165.
47. Ibid.
48. Ibid., 164.
49. Jay Taylor, *The Generalissimo's Son* (Cambridge: Harvard University Press, 2000), 290; Linda Chao and Ramon H. Myers, *The First Chinese Democracy* (Baltimore: Johns Hopkins University Press, 1998), 115–116.
50. Bush, 85.
51. Ibid., 90.
52. Ibid.
53. Ibid.
54. Ibid. Although the San Francisco Peace Treaty (1951)— the accord signed by 49 states formally ending the war with Japan—resulted in Japan renouncing its claims to Formosa, the treaty did not formally resolve the island's final status. The text of the treaty is available at: http://www.international.ucla.edu/eas/documents/peace1951.htm.
55. Bush, 92.
56. "Statement by Ambassador Bush in Plenary Session, October 25, 1971," USUN Press Release No. 168, reprinted as *U.S. State Department Bulletin* 65 (1971): 552–555.
57. "Full Text of Anti-Secession Law," *People's Daily Online*, March 14, 2005. Available at: http://english.people.com.cn/200503/14/eng20050314_176746.html. See Article 8 of the Anti-Secession Law, adopted at the Third Session of the Tenth National People's Congress.
58. "Bush Promises to Defend Taiwan as He Unveils Foreign Policy

Priorities," *The White House Bulletin*, November 19, 1999. Available at: http://www.fas.org/news/usa/1999/11/pr111999_nn.htm.

59. Secretary of State Condoleezza Rice, "Remarks at the Community of Democracies Opening Plenary," (Hyatt Regency Hotel, Santiago, Chile, April 28, 2005). Available at: http://www.state.gov/secretary/rm/2005/45386.htm.

60. President Bill Clinton, "Remarks by the President on China," (Johns Hopkins School for Advanced International Studies, March 8, 2000). Available at: http://www.clintonfoundation.org/legacy/030800-speech-by-president-on-china.htm.

SEVEN: WILL CHINA (CONTINUE TO) RISE?

1. See, inter alia, Angus Maddison, *Chinese Economic Performance In The Long Run*, (Paris: OECD, 1998), Dwight H. Perkins, *The Challenges of China's Growth*, (Washington, DC: AEI Press, 2006), and Eberhard Sandschneider, *Globale Rivalen: Chinas unheimlicher Ausstieg und die Ohnmacht des Westens*, (Munich: Hanser Verlag, 2007).

2. For example, U.S. National Intelligence Council, *Mapping The Global Future: Report of the National Intelligence Council's 2020 Project*, (Washington, DC: National Intelligence Council, 2004), available at: http://www.dni.gov/nic/NIC_globaltrend2020.html; U.S. Department of Defense, *Quadrennial Defense Review Report*, (Washington, DC: Department of Defense, 2006), available at: http://www.dni.gov/nic/NIC_globaltrend2020.html.

3. From 2003–2005, the formulation China's "peaceful rise" was in vogue in Chinese scholarly and official circles, and represented a widespread sense among Chinese elites of their country's long-term prospects. However, for a number of reasons—few of which having to do with any internal skepticism that China might continue to rise—the concept was dropped in favor of "peaceful development." For an interesting account of the history of the rise and fall of the concept of "peaceful rise," see Bonnie S. Glaser and Evan S. Medeiros, "The Changing Ecology of Foreign Policy-making in China: The Ascension and Demise of the Theory of 'Peaceful Rise,'" *China Quarterly* 190 (2007): 291–310. For a recent attempted

survey of Chinese opinion on their country's continued rise, see "The United States and the Rise of China and India: Results of a 2006 Multination Survey of Public Opinion," The Chicago Council on Global Affairs, 2006. Available at: www.thechicagocouncil.org/UserFiles/File/GlobalViews06Final.pdf.

4. Max H. Bazerman and Michael D. Watkins, *Predictable Surprises: The Disasters You Should Have Seen Coming, And How To Prevent Them* (Boston: Harvard Business School Press, 2004); Ian Bremmer, David Gordon, and Paul Bracken, eds., *Managing Strategic Surprise: Lessons from Risk Management and Risk Assessment* (New York: Eurasia Group Books, 2005).

5. Moreover, as my former AEI colleague Christopher Griffin has noted, the very concept of "the mandate of heaven"—that basic age-old cornerstone of Chinese political thought and regime legitimacy—is implicitly a theory about, and a justification for, the *end* of dominion by, and the demise of, Chinese states.

6. For example, Gordon H. Chang, *The Coming Collapse of China* (New York: Random House, 2001).

7. Any plausible scenario for a collapse of Communist China must, of course, recognize and take into account the observed differences between the Soviet-type totalitarian governments that have disappeared and the Chinese variant that endures. China's socialist tyranny has demonstrated immeasurably more resilience. This is, in a sense, where "softer" variants of the "collapsist" premises come into play: whereas "collapsist" scenarios contemplate discontinuities— even radical discontinuities—in China's international trajectory, the "softer" variants instead envision the troublesome factors they adduce as altering the angle and pace of this progression.

8. See, inter alia, Angus Maddison, *Chinese Economic Performance In The Long Run* (Paris: OECD, 1998); Dwight H. Perkins, *The Challenges of China's Growth* (Washington, DC: AEI Press, 2006).

9. Some benchmarks: Japan 1953–1973: 9.1 percent; Taiwan, 1962–1987: 9.6 percent; Hong Kong 1951–1981: 8.8 percent. Derived from Angus Maddison, *The World Economy: Historical Statistics* (Paris: OECD, 2003).

10. Charles Wolf et al., *Fault Lines in China's Economic Terrain* (Santa Monica: RAND Corporation, 2003).

11. Ibid., xxi.

12. For a careful but informative survey of this landscape from an administrative perspective, see OECD, *Governance in China* (Paris: OECD, 2005).

13. Willie Wo-Lap Lam, *Chinese Politics in the Hu Jintao Era* (Armonk, NY: M.E. Sharpe, 2006); Minxin Pei, *China's Trapped Transition: The Limits of Developmental Autocracy* (Cambridge: Harvard University Press, 2006).

14. Pei, 211–212.

15. For more on the methodological problems of attempting to predict big political changes in closed societies, see Nicholas Eberstadt, *The North Korean Economy Between Crisis and Catastrophe*, (New Brunswick: Transaction Publishers, 2007).

16. U.S. Census Bureau International Data Base, available electronically at http://www.census.gov/cgi-bin/ipc/idbagg.

17. For our purposes, the demographic horizon will extend to 2030—i.e., 21 years from now.

18. The two most frequently cited sources of global population projections are the aforementioned "International Data Base" from the U.S. Census Bureau and the UNPD "World Population Prospects" series. These are prepared independently, but in practice the UNPD's "medium variant" projection is usually very close to the Census Bureau's (single variant) projection. We will use Census and UNPD "medium variant" projections for China more or less interchangeably in this chapter, depending upon which aspect of China's prospective demographic changes we are attempting to illuminate.

19. These estimates, of course, are prepared under uncertainty: the most important of these being the lack of complete annual vital registration data for China, and the unknown degree of underreporting of infants and children in the country's censuses and demographic surveys. For background, see Daniel Goodkind, "China's missing children: The 2000 census underreporting surprise," *Population Studies* 58, no. 3 (2004): 281–295, and Guangyu Zhang and Zhonwei Zhao, "China's Fertility Puzzle: Data Collection and Data Use in the Last Two Decades," paper presented at Population Association of America 2005 Annual Meeting, Philadelpia, PA, April 1, 2005.

20. Cf. David Bloom and Jeffrey Williamson, "Demographic Transitions and Economic Miracles in Emerging Asia," *World Bank Economic Review* 12, no. 4 (1998): 419–456, David Bloom, David Canning, and Jose Sevilla, *The Demographic Dividend: A New Perspective on the Economic Consequences of Population Change* (Santa Monica: RAND Corporation, 2003).

21. Derived from China National Bureau of Statistics, *Tabulation on the 2000 Population Census of the People's Republic of China*, vol. II, Tables 4-4, 4-5.

22. Benjamin F. Jones, "Age and Great Invention," (NBER Working Papers # 11359, May 2005).

23. Some of these issues are thoughtfully addressed in Richard Jackson and Neil Howe, *The Graying of the Middle Kingdom* (Washington, DC: Center for Strategic and International Studies, 2004).

24. For background, see World Bank, *Old Age Security: Pension Reform in China* (Washington, DC: World Bank, 1997); Song Xiaowu, ed. *Perfect the Pension System* (Beijing: Enterprise Management Publishing House, 2001) [in Chinese]; Jinxing Huang, "Economic Restructuring, Social Safety-Net and Old-Age Pension Reform in China," *American Asian Review* 21, no. 2 (2003): 171–98; and Xin Wang, "China's Pension Reform and Capital Market Development," *China & World Economy* 12, no. 3 (2004): 3–16.

25. Data drawn from China Ministry of Labor and Social Security, *China Labour Statistical Yearbook 2003*, Tables 1-43, 1-51, and China National Bureau of Statistics, *Tabulation on the 2000 Population Census of the People's Republic of China*, Vol. 2, Tables 4-4, 4-4c.

26. Li Bohua, "Level, Trends and Determinants of Fertility in China: 1973–1987,"*Asia-Pacific Population Journal* 5, no. 2 (1990): 2–16.

27. Gu Baochang, "Lower Fertility in China: Trends, Policy and Impact" (working paper, prepared for the Seminar on Fertility Transition in Asia: Opportunities and Challenges, December 18–20, 2006, Bangkok). Available at: http://www.unescap.org/esid/psis/meetings/FertilityTransition/Gu-China%20_SFTA10.pdf.

28. Dwight H. Perkins, "Law, Family Ties, and the East Asian Way of Business," in *Culture Matters: How Values Shape Human Progress*, *eds.* Lawrence E. Harrison and Samuel P. Huntington (New York: Basic Books, 2000), 232–243.

29. These scenarios comport with the ones outlined in Minxin Pei, "China: Can Economic Growth Continue Without Political Reform?" in *Strategic Asia 2006/07: Trade, Interdependence and Security*, eds. Ashley J. Tellis and Michael Wills (Seattle: National Bureau of Asian Research, 2006), 303–331.

30. Passages in the following section are drawn from Nicholas Eberstadt, "Critical Cross-Cutting Issues Facing Northeast Asia: Regional Demographic Trends and Prospects," *Asia Policy*, no. 3 (2007): 48–56, and Nicholas Eberstadt., "Strategic Implications of Asian Demographic Trends," in *Strategic Asia: 2003/2004*, eds. Aaron L. Friedberg, Richard J. Ellings, and Michael Wills (Seattle: National Bureau of Asian Research, 2003), 454–84.

31. Daniel Goodkind, "Recent trends in the sex ratio at birth in East Asia" (unpublished working paper, U.S. Bureau of the Census, International Programs Center, June 2002).

32. *China Statistical Yearbook 2006*, Table 4-7. Available at: http://www. stats.gov.cn/tjsj/ndsj/2006/indexeh.htm.

33. William Hurst and Kevin J. O'Brien, "China's Contentious Pensioners," *China Quarterly* 170 (2002): 345–360.

34. Population Division of the Department of Economic and Social Affairs of the United Nations Secretariat, *World Population Prospects. The 2004 Revision*, and *World Urbanization Prospects: The 2005 Revision*, available at http://esa.un.org/unup.

35. The floating population here is defined as "individuals who have resided at the place of destination for at least six months without local household registration status" that cross county boundaries. See Zai Liang and Zhongdong Ma, "China's Floating Population: New Evidence from the 2000 Census," *Population and Development Review* 30, no. 3 (2004): 467–488.

36. Daniel Goodkind and Loraine A. West, "China's Floating Population: Definitions, Data and Recent Findings," *Urban Studies* 39, no. 12 (2002): 2237–2250. Note that the duration of stay is undefined.

37. Zai Liang and Zhongdong Ma, "China's Floating Population: New Evidence from the 2000 Census," *Population and Development Review* 30, no. 3 (2004): 467–488.

INDEX